Charles Godfrey Leland

Abraham Lincoln and the Abolition of Slavery in the United States

Charles Godfrey Leland

Abraham Lincoln and the Abolition of Slavery in the United States

ISBN/EAN: 9783744718240

Printed in Europe, USA, Canada, Australia, Japan

Cover: Foto ©Suzi / pixelio.de

More available books at **www.hansebooks.com**

ABRAHAM LINCOLN

AND THE

ABOLITION OF SLAVERY IN THE UNITED STATES

BY

CHARLES GODFREY LELAND

AUTHOR OF "HANS BREITMANN'S BALLADS," "THE EGYPTIAN SKETCH BOOK,"
ETC., ETC.

NEW YORK
G. P. PUTNAM'S SONS
182 FIFTH AVENUE
1879

PUBLISHERS' NOTE.

IN issuing this second edition of Mr. Leland's biography, the publishers have taken occasion to correct a few errors in dates and proper names, and in citations from documents, that had crept into the first edition.

The book was prepared during the author's residence abroad, where he did not have at hand for reference all the authorities needed, and as it was stereotyped in London the above oversights were not at once detected.

PREFACE.

I MAKE no apology for adding another "Life of Abraham Lincoln" to the many already written, as I believe it impossible to make such an example of successful perseverance allied to honesty, as the great President gave, too well known to the world. And as I know of no other man whose life shows so perfectly what may be effected by resolute self-culture, and adherence to good principles in spite of obstacles, I infer that such an example cannot be too extensively set before all young men who are ambitious to do *well* in the truest sense. There are also other reasons why it should be studied. The life of Abraham Lincoln during his Presidency is simply that of his country—since he was so intimately concerned with every public event of his time, that as sometimes happens with photographs, so with the biography of Lincoln and the history of his time, we cannot decide whether the great picture was enlarged from the smaller one, or the smaller reduced from a greater. His career also fully proves that extremes meet, since in no despotism is there an example of any one who ever governed so great a country so thoroughly in detail as did this Republican of Republicans, whose one thought was simply to obey the people.

It is of course impossible to give within the limits of a small book all the details of a busy life, and also the history of the American Emancipation and its causes; but I trust that I have omitted little of much importance. The books to which I have been chiefly indebted, and from which I have borrowed most freely, are the lives of Lincoln by W. H. Lamon, and by my personal friends H. J. Raymond and Dr. Holland; and also the works referring to the war by I. N. Arnold, F. B. Carpenter, L. P. Brockett, A. Boyd, G. W. Bacon, J. Barrett, Adam Badeau, and F. Moore.

C. G. L.

June, 1879.

CONTENTS.

CHAPTER I.

Birth of Abraham Lincoln—The Lincoln Family—Abraham's first Schooling—Death of Mrs. Lincoln, and the new "Mother"—Lincoln's Boyhood and Youth—Self-Education—Great Physical Strength—First Literary Efforts—Journey to New Orleans—Encouraging Incident, ... 9

CHAPTER II.

Lincoln's Appearance—His First Public Speech—Again at New Orleans—Mechanical Genius—Clerk in a Country Store—Elected Captain—The Black Hawk War—Is a successful Candidate for the Legislature—Becomes a Storekeeper, Land Surveyor, and Postmaster—His First Love—The "Long Nine"—First Step towards Emancipation, ... 30

CHAPTER III.

Lincoln settles at Springfield as a Lawyer—Candidate for the office of Presidential Elector—A Love Affair—Marries Miss Todd—Religious Views—Exerts himself for Henry Clay—Elected to Congress in 1846—Speeches in Congress—Out of Political Employment until 1854—Anecdotes of Lincoln as a Lawyer, ... 53

CHAPTER IV.

Rise of the Southern Party—Formation of the Abolition and the Free Soil Parties—Judge Douglas and the Kansas-Nebraska Bill—Douglas defeated by Lincoln—Lincoln resigns as Candidate for Congress—Lincoln's Letter on Slavery—The Bloomington Speech—The Fremont Campaign—Election of Buchanan—The Dred-Scott Decision, ... 64

CHAPTER V.

Causes of Lincoln's Nomination to the Presidency—His Lectures in New York, &c.—The First Nomination and the Fence Rails—The Nomination at Chicago—Elected President—Office-seekers and Appointments—Lincoln's Impartiality—The South determined to Secede—Fears for Lincoln's Life, ... 78

CHAPTER VI.

A Suspected Conspiracy—Lincoln's Departure for Washington—His Speeches at Springfield and on the road to the National Capital—Breaking out of the Rebellion—Treachery of President Buchanan—Treason in the Cabinet—Jefferson Davis's Message—Threats of Massacre and Ruin to the North—Southern Sympathisers—Lincoln's Inaugural Address—The Cabinet—The Days of Doubt and of Darkness, ... 88

CHAPTER VII.

Mr. Seward refuses to meet the Rebel Commissioners—Lincoln's Forbearance—Fort Sumter—Call for 75,000 Troops—Troubles in Maryland—Administrative Prudence—Judge Douglas—Increase of the Army—Winthrop and Ellsworth—Bull Run—General M'Clellan, 102

CHAPTER VIII.

Relations with Europe—Foreign Views of the War—The Slaves—Proclamation of Emancipation—Arrest of Rebel Commissioners—Black Troops, ... 117

CHAPTER IX.

Eighteen Hundred and Sixty-two—The Plan of the War, and Strength of the Armies—General M'Clellan—The General Movement, January 27th, 1862—The brilliant Western Campaign—Removal of M'Clellan—The *Monitor*—Battle of Fredericksburg—Vallandigham and Seymour—The *Alabama*—President Lincoln declines all Foreign Mediation, ... 134

CHAPTER X.

Eighteen Hundred and Sixty-three—A Popular Prophecy—General Burnside relieved and General Hooker appointed—Battle of Chancellorsville—The Rebels invade Pennsylvania—Battle of Gettysburg—Lincoln's Speech at Gettysburg—Grant takes Vicksburg—Port Hudson—Battle of Chattanooga—New York Riots—The French in Mexico—Troubles in Missouri, ... 147

CHAPTER XI.

Proclamation of Amnesty—Lincoln's Benevolence—His Self-reliance—Progress of the Campaign—The Summer of 1864—Lincoln's Speech at Philadelphia—Suffering in the South—Raids—Sherman's March—Grant's Position—Battle of the Wilderness—Siege of Petersburg—Chambersburg—Naval Victories—Confederate Intrigues—Presidential Election—Lincoln Re-elected—Atrocious Attempts of the Confederates, ... 172

CHAPTER XII.

The President's Reception of Negroes—The South opens Negotiations for Peace—Proposals—Lincoln's Second Inauguration—The Last Battle—Davis Captured—End of the War—Death of Lincoln—Public Mourning, ... 203

CHAPTER XIII.

President Lincoln's Characteristics—His Love of Humour—His Stories—Pithy Sayings—Repartees—His Dignity, . . . 233

INDEX, ... 245

LIFE OF ABRAHAM LINCOLN.

CHAPTER I.

Birth of Abraham Lincoln—The Lincoln Family—Abraham's first Schooling—Death of Mrs. Lincoln, and the new "Mother"—Lincoln's Boyhood and Youth—Self-Education—Great Physical Strength—First Literary Efforts—Journey to New Orleans—Encouraging Incident.

ABRAHAM LINCOLN was born in Kentucky, on the 12th day of February, 1809. The log-cabin which was his birth-place was built on the south branch of Nolin's Creek, three miles from the village of Hodgensville, on land which was then in the county of Hardin, but is now included in that of La Rue. His father, Thomas Lincoln, was born in 1778; his mother's maiden name was Nancy Hanks. The Lincoln family, which appears to have been of unmixed English descent, came to Kentucky from Berks County, Pennsylvania, to which place tradition or conjecture asserts they had emigrated from Massachusetts. But they did not remain long in Pennsylvania, since they seem to have gone before 1752 to Rockingham, County Virginia, which state was then one with that of Kentucky. There is, however, so much doubt as to these details of their early history, that it is not certain whether they were at first emigrants directly from England to Virginia, an offshoot of the historic Lincoln family in Massachusetts, or of the highly respectable Lincolns of Pennsylvania.[1] This obscurity is plainly due to the great poverty and lowly station of the Virginian Lincolns. "My parents," said President Lincoln, in a brief autobiographic sketch,[2] "were both born of undistinguished families — second families, perhaps, I should say." To this he adds that his paternal grandfather was Abraham Lincoln, who migrated from Rockingham, County Virginia, to Kentucky, "about 1781 or 2," although his cousins and other relatives all declare this grandsire's name to have been Mordecai—a striking proof of the ignorance and indifference of the family respecting matters seldom neglected.

This grandfather, Abraham or Mordecai, having removed to Kentucky, "the dark and bloody ground," settled in Mercer County. Their house was a rough log-cabin, their farm a little clearing in the midst of the forest. One morning, not long after their settlement, the father took Thomas, his youngest son, and went to build a fence a short distance from the house,

---

[1] Lamon, c. i. p. 1.   [2] Addressed to J. W. Fell, March, 1872.

while the other brothers, Mordecai and Josiah, were sent to a field not far away. They were all intent upon their work, when a shot from a party of Indians in ambush was heard. The father fell dead. Josiah ran to a stockade, or settlement, two or three miles off; Mordecai, the eldest boy, made his way to the house, and, looking out from a loop-hole, saw an Indian in the act of raising his little brother from the ground. He took deliberate aim at a silver ornament on the breast of the Indian, and brought him down. Thomas sprang towards the cabin, and was admitted by his mother, while Mordecai renewed his fire at several other Indians who rose from the covert of the fence, or thicket. It was not long before Josiah returned from the stockade with a party of settlers; but the Indians had fled, and none were found but the dead one, and another who was wounded, and had crept into the top of a fallen tree. Mordecai, it is said, hated the Indians ever after with an intensity which was unusual even in those times. As Allan Macaulay, in "Waverley," is said to have hunted down the Children of the Mist, or as the Quaker Nathan, in Bird's romance of "Nick of the Woods," is described as hunting the Shawnese, so we are told this other avenger of blood pursued his foes with unrelenting, unscrupulous hatred. For days together he would follow peaceable Indians as they passed through the settlements, in order to get secret shots at them.[1]

Mordecai, the Indian-killer, and his brother, Josiah, remained in Virginia, and grew up to be respectable, prosperous men. The younger brother, Thomas, was always "idle, thriftless, poor, a hunter, and a rover." He exercised occasionally in a rough way the calling of a carpenter, and, wandering from place to place, began at different times to cultivate the wilderness, but with little success, owing to his laziness. Yet he was a man of great strength and vigour, and once "thrashed the monstrous bully of Breckinridge County in three minutes, and came off without a scratch." He was an inveterate talker, or popular teller of stories and anecdotes, and a Jackson Democrat in politics, which signified that he belonged to the more radical of the two political parties which then prevailed in America. In religion, he was, says Lamon, who derived his information from Mr. W. H. Herndon, "nothing at times, and a member of various denominations by turns." In 1806, he lived at Elizabethtown, in Hardin County, Kentucky, where, in the same year and place, he married Nancy Hanks: the exact date of the marriage is unknown. It is said of this young woman that she was a tall and beautiful brunette,

---

[1] Lamon, p. 7.

with an understanding which, by her family at least, was considered wonderful. She could read and write—as rare accomplishments in those days in Kentucky backwoods as they still are among the poor whites of the South or their Western descendants.[1] In later life she was sadly worn by hard labour, both in the house and fields, and her features were marked with a melancholy which was probably constitutional, and which her son inherited.

It is to be regretted that President Abraham Lincoln never spoke, except with great reluctance, of his early life, or of his parents. As it is, the researches of W. H. Herndon and others have indicated the hereditary sources of his chief characteristics. We know that the grandfather was a vigorous backwoodsman, who died a violent death; that his uncle was a grim and determined manslayer, carrying out for years the blood-feud provoked by the murder of his parent; that his mother was habitually depressed, and that his father was a favourite of both men and women, though a mere savage when irritated, fond of fun, an endless storyteller, physically powerful, and hating hard work. Out of all these preceding traits, it is not difficult

---

[1] In 1865, I saw many companies and a few regiments "mustered out" in Nashville, Tennessee. In the most intelligent companies, only one man in eight or nine could sign his name. Fewer still could read. —C. G. L.

to imagine how the giant Abraham came to be inflexible of purpose and strong of will, though indolent—why he was good-natured to excess in his excess of strength—and why he was a great humourist, and at the same time a melancholy man.

It should be remembered by the reader that the state of society in which Abraham Lincoln was born and grew up resembled nothing now existing in Europe, and that it is very imperfectly understood even by many town-dwelling Americans. The people around him were all poor and ignorant, yet they bore their poverty lightly, were hardly aware of their want of culture, and were utterly unconscious of owing the least respect or deference to any human being. Some among them were, of course, aware of the advantages to be derived from wealth and political power; but the majority knew not how to spend the one, and were indifferent to the other. Even to this day, there are in the South and South-West scores of thousands of men who, owning vast tracts of fertile land, and gifted with brains and muscle, will not take the pains to build themselves homes better than ordinary cabins, or cultivate more soil than will supply life with plain and unvaried sustenance. The only advantage they have is the inestimable one, if properly treated, of being free from all trammels save those of ignorance. To rightly appreciate the good or evil qualities of men moulded in such society, requires great generosity, and great freedom from all that is conventional.

Within the first few years of her married life, Nancy Hanks Lincoln bore her husband three children. The first was a daughter, named Sarah, who married at fifteen, and died soon after; the second was Abraham; and the third Thomas, who died in infancy.[1] The family were always wretchedly poor, even below the level of their neighbours in want; and as the father was indolent, the wife was obliged to labour and suffer. But it is probable that Mrs. Lincoln, who could read, and Thomas, who attributed his failure in life to ignorance, wished their children to be educated. Schools were, of course, scarce in a country where the houses are often many miles apart. Zachariah Riney, a Catholic priest, was Abraham's first teacher; his next was Caleb Hazel. The young pupil learned to read and write in a few weeks; but in all his life, reckoning his instruction by days, he had only one year's schooling.

When Thomas Lincoln was first married (1806), he took his wife to live in Elizabethtown, in a wretched shed, which has since been used as a slaughter-house and stable. About a year after, he removed to Nolin's Creek. Four years after the

---

[1] J. G. Holland, p. 22.

birth of Abraham (1809), he again migrated to a more picturesque and fertile place, a few miles distant on Knob Creek. Here he remained four years, and though he was the occupant of over 200 acres of good land, never cultivated more than a little patch, "being satisfied with milk and meal for food." When his children went to school they walked eight miles, going and returning, having only maize bread for dinner. In 1816, the father, after having sold his interest in the farm for ten barrels of whiskey and twenty dollars, built himself a crazy flat-boat, and set sail alone on the Ohio, seeking for a new home. By accident, the boat foundered, and much of the cargo was lost; but Thomas Lincoln pushed on, and found a fitting place to settle in Indiana, near the spot on which the village of Gentryville now stands. It was in the untrodden wilderness, and here he soon after brought his family, to live for the first year in what is called a half-faced camp, or a rough hut of poles, of which only three sides were enclosed, the fourth being open to the air. In 1817, Betsy Sparrow, an aunt of Mrs. Lincoln, and her husband, Thomas, with a nephew named Dennis Hanks, joined the Lincolns, who removed to a better house, if that could be called a house which was built of rough logs, and had neither floor, door, nor window. For two years they continued to live in this manner. Lincoln, a carpenter, was too lazy to make himself the simplest furniture. They had a few three-legged stools; the only bed was made in a singular manner. Its head and one side were formed by a corner of the cabin, the bed-post was a single crotch cut from the forest. Laid upon this crotch were the ends of two hickory poles, whose other extremities were placed in two holes made in the logs of the wall. On these sticks rested "slats," or boards rudely split from trees with an axe, and on these slats was laid a bag filled with dried leaves. This was the bed of Thomas and Nancy Lincoln, and into it—when the skins hung at the cabin entrance did not keep out the cold—little Abraham and his sister crept for warmth.[1] Very little is recorded of the childhood of the future President. He was once nearly drowned in a stream, and when eight years of age shot a wild turkey, which, he declared in after life, was the largest game he had ever killed—a remarkable statement for a man who had grown up in a deer country, where buck-skin formed the common material for clothing, and venison hams passed for

---

[1] J. G. Holland, "Life of Lincoln," p. 28. The children probably slept on the earth. The writer has seen a man, owning hundreds of acres of rich bottom land, living in a log-hut, nearly such as is here described. There was only a single stool, an iron pot, a knife, and a gun in the cabin, but no bedstead, the occupant and his wife sleeping in two cavities in the dirt-floor. Such had been their home for years.

money. One thing is at least certain—that, till he was ten years old, the poor boy was ill-clad, dirty, and ill-used by his father. He had, however, learned to write.

In 1818, a terrible but common epidemic, known in Western America as the milk-fever, broke out in Indiana, and within a few days Thomas and Betsy Sparrow and Mrs. Lincoln all died. They had no medical attendance, and it was nine months before a clergyman, named David Elkin, invited by the first letter which Abraham ever wrote, came one hundred miles to hold the funeral service and preach over the graves. Strange as it may seem, the event which is universally regarded as the saddest of every life, in the case of Abraham Lincoln led directly to greater happiness, and to a change which conduced to the development of all his better qualities. Thirteen months after the death of Nancy Lincoln, Thomas married a widow, Mrs. Johnston, whom he had wooed ineffectually in Kentucky when she was Miss Sally Bush. She was a woman of sense, industrious, frugal, and gifted with a pride which inspired her to lead a far more civilised life than that which satisfied poor Tom Lincoln. He had greatly exaggerated to her the advantages of his home in Indiana, and she was bitterly disappointed when they reached it. Fortunately, she owned a stock of good furniture, which greatly astonished little Abraham and Sarah and their cousin Dennis. "She set about mending matters with great energy, and made her husband put down a floor, and hang windows and doors." It was in the depth of winter, and the children, as they nestled in the warm beds she had provided, enjoying the strange luxury of security from the cold winds of December, must have thanked her from the depths of their hearts. She had brought a son and two daughters of her own, but Abraham and his sister had an equal place in her affections. They were half naked, and she clad them; they were dirty, and she washed them; they had been ill-used, and she treated them with motherly tenderness. In her own language, she "made them look a little more human."[1]

This excellent woman loved Abraham tenderly, and her love was warmly returned. After his death she declared to Mr. Herndon—"I can say what not one mother in ten thousand can of a boy—Abe never gave me a cross look, and never refused, in fact or appearance, to do anything I requested him; nor

---

[1] Lamon, vol. i., pp. 31 and 40. Abraham's father is said by Dennis Hanks (from whom Mr. Herndon, Lamon's authority, derived much information) to have loved his son, but it is certain that, at the same time, he treated him very cruelly. Hanks admits that he had several times seen little Abraham knocked headlong from the fence by his father, while civilly answering questions put by travellers as to their way.

did I ever give him a cross word in all my life. His mind and mine—what little I had—seemed to run together. He was dutiful to me always. Abe was the best boy I ever saw, or ever expect to see."
"When in after years Mr. Lincoln spoke of his 'saintly mother,' and of his 'angel of a mother,' he referred to this noble woman, who first made him feel 'like a human being'—whose goodness first touched his childish heart, and taught him that blows and taunts and degradation were not to be his only portion in the world." And if it be recorded of George Washington that he never told a lie, it should also be remembered of Abraham Lincoln, who carried his country safely through a greater crisis than that of the Revolutionary War,[1] that he always obeyed his mother.

Abraham had gone to school only a few weeks in Kentucky, and Mrs. Lincoln soon sent him again to receive instruction. His first teacher in Indiana was Hazel Dorsey; his next, Andrew Crawford. The latter, in addition to the ordinary branches of education, also taught "manners." One scholar would be introduced by another, while walking round

---

[1] W. H. Herndon, who was for many years the law-partner of Abraham Lincoln, in a letter to me, written not long after the murder of his old friend, earnestly asserted his opinion that the late President was a greater man than General Washington, founding his opinion on the greater difficulties which he subdued.—C. G. L.

the log schoolroom, to all the boys and girls, taught to bow properly, and otherwise acquire the ordinary courtesies of life. Abraham distinguished himself in spelling, which has always been a favourite subject for competition in rural America, and he soon began to write short original articles, though composition formed no part of the studies. It was characteristic of the boy that his first essays were against cruelty to animals. His mates were in the habit of catching the box-turtles, or land-terrapins, or tortoises, and putting live coals on their backs to make them walk, which greatly annoyed Abraham. All who knew him, in boyhood or in later life, bear witness that his tenderness was equal to his calm courage and tremendous physical strength. The last school which he attended for a short time, and to reach which he walked every day nine miles, was kept by a Mr. Swaney. This was in 1826.

Abraham was now sixteen years of age, and had grown so rapidly that he had almost attained the height which he afterwards reached of six feet four inches. He was very dark, his skin was shrivelled even in boyhood by constant exposure, and he habitually wore low shoes, a linsey-woolsey shirt, a cap made from the skin of a raccoon or opossum, and buckskin breeches, which were invariably about twelve inches too short for him. When not working for his father, he was hired out as a farm-labourer to the neighbours. His cousin, John Hanks, says—"We worked barefoot, grubbed it, ploughed, mowed, and cradled together."

All who knew him at this time testify that Abraham hated hard-work, though he did it well—that he was physically indolent, though intellectually very active—that he loved to laugh, tell stories, and joke while labouring—and that he passed his leisure moments in hard study or in reading, which he made hard by writing out summaries of all he read, and getting them by heart. He would study arithmetic at night by the light of the fire, and cipher or copy with a pencil or coal on the wooden shovel or on a board. When this was full, he would shave it off with his father's drawing-knife, and begin again. When he had paper, he used it instead; but in the frequent intervals when he had none, the boards were kept until paper was obtained. Among the first books which he read and thoroughly mastered were "Æsop's Fables," "Robinson Crusoe," Bunyan's "Pilgrim's Progress," a "History of the United States," Weem's "Life of Washington," and "The Revised Statutes of Indiana." From another work, "The Kentucky Preceptor," a collection of literary extracts, he is said by a Mrs. Crawford, who knew him well, to have "learned his school orations, speeches, and pieces to write." The field-work, which Abraham Lincoln disliked, did not, however, exhaust his body, and his mind found relief after toil in mastering anything in print.[1] It is not unusual to see poor and ignorant youths who are determined to "get learning," apply themselves to the hardest and dryest intellectual labour with very little discrimination of any difference between that and more attractive literature, and it is evident that young Lincoln worked in this spirit. There is no proof that his memory was by nature extraordinary—it would rather seem that the contrary was the case, from the pains which he took to improve it. During his boyhood, any book had to him all the charm of rarity; perhaps it was the more charming because most of his friends believed that mental culture was incompatible with industry. "Lincoln," said his cousin, Dennis Hanks, "was lazy—a very lazy man. He was always reading, scribbling, writing, ciphering, writing poetry, and the like." It is evident that his custom of continually exercising his memory on all subjects grew with his growth and strengthened with his strength. By the time he was twenty-five, he had, without instruction, made himself a good lawyer—not a mere "case-practitioner," but one who argued from a sound knowledge of principles. It is said that when he began to read Blackstone, he thoroughly learned the first forty pages at one

---

[1] "Abraham's poverty of books was the wealth of his life."—J. G. HOLLAND.

sitting. There is also sufficient proof that he had perfectly mastered not only "Euclid's Geometry," but a number of elementary scientific works, among others one on astronomy. And many anecdotes of his later life prove that he learned nothing without thinking it over deeply, especially in all its relations to his other acquisitions and its practical use. If education consists of mental discipline and the acquisition of knowledge, it is idle to say that Abraham Lincoln was uneducated, since few college graduates actually excelled him in either respect. These facts deserve dwelling on, since, in the golden book of self-made men, there is not one who presents a more encouraging example to youth, and especially to the poor and ambitious, than Abraham Lincoln. He developed his memory by resolutely training it—he brought out his reasoning powers as a lawyer by using his memory—he became a fluent speaker and a ready reasoner by availing himself of every opportunity to speak or debate. From the facts which have been gathered by his biographers, or which are current in conversation among those who knew him, it is most evident that there seldom lived a man who owed so little to innate genius or talents, in comparison to what he achieved by sheer determination and perseverance.

When Abraham was fifteen or sixteen, he began to exercise his memory in a new direction, by frequenting not only religious but political meetings, and by mounting the stump of a tree the day after and repeating with great accuracy all he had heard. It is said that he mimicked with great skill not only the tones of preachers and orators, but also their gestures and facial expressions. Anything like cruelty to man or beast would always inspire him to an original address, in which he would preach vigorously against inflicting pain. Wherever he spoke an audience was sure to assemble, and as this frequently happened in the harvest-field, the youthful orator or actor was often dragged down by his angry father and driven to his work. His wit and humour, his inexhaustible fund of stories, and, above all, his kind heart, made him everywhere a favourite. Women, says Mr. Lamon, were especially pleased, for he was always ready to do any kind of work for them, such as chopping wood, making a fire, or nursing a baby. Any family was glad when he was hired to work with them, since he did his work well, and made them all merry while he was about it. In 1825, he was employed by James Taylor as a ferry-man, to manage a boat which crossed the Ohio and Anderson's Creek. In addition to this he worked on the farm, acted as hostler, ground corn, built the fires, put the water early on the fire, and prepared for the mistress's cooking. Though he was obliged to rise so early, he always studied till nearly midnight. He was in great demand when hogs were slaughtered. For this rough work he was paid 31 cents (about 16d.) a-day. Meanwhile, he became incredibly strong. He could carry six hundred pounds with ease; he once picked up some huge posts which four men were about to lift, and bore them away with little effort. Men yet alive have seen him lift a full barrel of liquor and drink from the bung-hole. "He could sink an axe," said an old friend, "deeper into wood than any man I ever saw." He was especially skilled in wrestling, and from the year 1828 there was no man, far or near, who would compete with him in it.[1] From his boyhood, he was extremely temperate. Those who have spoken most freely of his faults admit that, in a country where a whiskey-jug was kept in every house, Lincoln never touched spirits except to avoid giving offence. His stepmother thought he was temperate to a fault.

Meanwhile, as the youth grew apace, the neighbouring village of Gentryville had grown with him. Books and cultivated society became more accessible. The great man of the place was a Mr. Jones, the storekeeper, whose shop supplied all kinds of goods required by farmers. Mr. Jones took a liking to young Lincoln, employed him sometimes, taught

---

[1] Lamon, p. 54.

him politics, giving him deep impressions in favour of Andrew Jackson, the representative of the Democratic party, and finally awoke Abraham's ambition by admiring him, and predicting that he would some day be a great man. Another friend was John Baldwin, the village blacksmith, who was, even for a Western American wag, wonderfully clever at a jest, and possessed of an inexhaustible fund of stories. It was from John Baldwin that Lincoln derived a great number of the quaint anecdotes with which he was accustomed in after years to illustrate his arguments. His memory contained thousands of these drolleries; so that, eventually, there was no topic of conversation which did not "put him in mind of a little story." In some other respects, his acquisitions were less useful. Though he knew a vast number of ballads, he could not sing one; and though a reader of Burns, certain of his own satires and songs, levelled at some neighbours who had slighted him, were mere doggerel, wanting every merit, and very bitter. But, about 1827, he contributed an article on temperance and another on American politics to two newspapers, published in Ohio. From the praise awarded by a lawyer, named Pritchard, to the political article, it would appear to have been very well written. Even in this first essay in politics, Lincoln urged the principle by which he became famous, and for which he died—

adherence to the constitution and the integrity of the American Union.

In March, 1828, Abraham Lincoln was hired by Mr. Gentry, the proprietor of Gentryville, as "bow-hand," and "to work the front oars," on a boat going with a cargo of bacon to New Orleans. This was a trip of 1800 miles, and then, as now, the life of an Ohio and Mississippi boatman was full of wild adventure. One incident which befel the future President was sufficiently strange. Having arrived at a sugar-plantation six miles below Baton Rouge, the boat was pulled in, and Lincoln, with his companion, a son of Mr. Gentry, went to sleep. Hearing footsteps in the night, they sprang up, and saw that a gang of seven negroes were coming on board to rob or murder. Seizing a hand-spike, Lincoln rushed towards them, and as the leader jumped on the boat, knocked him into the water. The second, third, and fourth, as they leaped aboard, were served in the same way, and the others fled, but were pursued by Lincoln and Gentry, who inflicted on them a severe beating. In this encounter, Abraham received a wound the scar of which he bore through life. It is very probable that among these negroes who would have taken the life of the future champion of emancipation, there were some who lived to share its benefits and weep for his death.[1]

---

[1] Holland and Lamon.

It was during this voyage, or about this time, that two strangers paid Abraham half a silver dollar each for rowing them ashore in a boat. Relating this to Mr. Seward, Secretary of State, he said—"You may think it was a very little thing, but it was a most important incident in my life. I could scarcely believe that I, a poor boy, had earned a dollar in less than a day. I was a more hopeful and confident being from that time."

CHAPTER II.

Lincoln's Appearance—His First Public Speech—Again at New Orleans—Mechanical Genius—Clerk in a Country Store—Elected Captain—The Black Hawk War—Is a successful Candidate for the Legislature—Becomes a Storekeeper, Land-Surveyor, and Postmaster—His First Love—The "Long Nine"—First Step towards Emancipation.

IN 1830, Thomas Lincoln had again tired of his home, and resolved to move Westward. This time he did not change without good reason: an epidemic had appeared in his Indiana neighbourhood, which was besides generally unhealthy. Therefore, in the spring, he and Abraham, with Dennis Hanks and Levi Hall, who had married one of Mrs. Lincoln's daughters by her first husband, with their families, thirteen in all, having packed their furniture on a waggon, drawn by four oxen, took the road for Illinois. After journeying 200 miles in fifteen days, Thomas Lincoln settled in Moron County, on the Sangamon River, about ten miles west of Decatur. Here they built a cabin of hewn timber, with a smoke-house for drying meat, and a stable, and broke up and fenced fifteen acres of land.

Abraham Lincoln was now twenty-one, and his father had been a hard master, taking all his wages. He therefore, after doing his best to settle the family in their new home, went forth to work for himself among the farmers. One George Cluse, who worked with Abraham during the first year in Illinois, says that at that time he was "the roughest-looking person he ever saw: he was tall, angular, and ungainly, and wore trousers of flax and tow, cut tight at the ankle and out at the knees. He was very poor, and made a bargain with Mrs. Nancy Miller to split 400 rails for every yard of brown jean, dyed with walnut bark, that would be required to make him a pair of trousers."

Thomas Lincoln found, in less than a year, that his new home was the most unhealthy of all he had tried. So he went Westward again, moving to three new places until he settled at Goose Nest Prairie, in Coles County, where he died at the age of seventy-three, "as usual, in debt." From the time of his death, and as he advanced in prosperity, Abraham aided his stepmother in many ways besides sending her money. It was at Decatur that he made his first public speech, standing on a keg. It was on the navigation of the Sangamon River, and was delivered extemporaneously in reply to one by a candidate for the Legislature, named Posey.

During the winter of 1831, a trader, named Denton Offutt, proposed to John Hanks, Abraham Lincoln, and John D. Johnston, his stepmother's son, to take a flat-boat to New Orleans. The wages offered were very high—fifty cents a day to each man, and sixty dollars to be divided among them at the end of the trip. After some delay, the boat, loaded with corn, pigs, and pork, sailed, but just below New Salem, on the Sangamon, it stuck on a dam, but was saved by the great ingenuity of Lincoln, who invented a novel apparatus for getting it over. This seems to have turned his mind to the subject of overcoming such difficulties of navigation, and in 1849 he obtained a patent for "an improved method of lifting vessels over shoals." The design is a bellows attached to each side of the hull, below the water-line, to be pumped full of air when it is desired to lift the craft over a shoal. The model, which is eighteen or twenty inches long, and which is now in the Patent Office at Washington, appears to have been cut with a knife from a shingle and a cigar-box.[1] John Hanks, apparently a most trustworthy and excellent man, declared that it was during this trip, while at New Orleans, Lincoln first saw negroes chained, maltreated, and whipped. It made a deep impression on his humane mind, and, years after, he often declared that witnessing this cruelty first induced him to think slavery wrong. At New Orleans the flat-boat discharged its cargo, and was sold for its timber. Lincoln returned on a steamboat

---

[1] *Vide* Ripley and Dana's "Cyclopædia;" also, article from the Boston "Commercial Advertiser," cited by Lamon.

to St. Louis, and thence walked home. He had hardly returned, before he received a challenge from a famous wrestler, named Daniel Needham. There was a great assembly at Wabash Point, to witness the match, where Needham was thrown with so much ease that his pride was more hurt than his body.

In July, 1831, Abraham again engaged himself to Mr. Offutt, to take charge of a country store at New Salem. While awaiting his employer, an election was held, and a clerk was wanted at the polls. The stranger, Abraham, being asked whether he was competent to fill the post, said, "I will try," and performed the duties well. This was the first public official act of his life; and as soon as Offutt's goods arrived, Lincoln, from a day-labourer, became a clerk, or rather salesman, in which capacity he remained for one year, or until the spring of 1832, when his employer failed. Many incidents are narrated of Lincoln's honesty towards customers during this clerkship—of his strict integrity in trifles —his bravery when women were annoyed by bullies— and of his prowess against a gang of ruffians who infested and ruled the town. He is said to have more than once walked several miles after business hours to return six cents, or some equally trifling sum, when he had been overpaid. It is very evident that he managed all matters with so much tact as
c

to make fast friends of everybody, and was specially a favourite of the men with whom he fought. It was now that he began to cultivate popularity, quietly, but with the same determination which he had shown in acquiring knowledge. To his credit be it said, that he effected this neither by flattery nor servility, but by making the most of his good qualities, and by inducing respect for his honesty, intelligence, and bravery. It is certain that, during a year, Mr. Offutt was continually stimulating his ambition, and insisting that he knew more than any man in the United States, and would some day be President. Lincoln himself knew very well by this time of what stuff many of the men were made who rose in politics, and that, with a little luck and perseverance, he could hold his own with them. When out of the "store," he was always busy, as of old, in the pursuit of knowledge. He mastered the English grammar, remarking that, "if that was what they called a science, he thought he could subdue another." A Mr. Green, who became his fellow-clerk, declares that his talk now showed that he was beginning to think of "a great life and a great destiny." He busied himself very much with debating clubs, walking many miles to attend them, and for years continued to take the "Louisville Journal," famous for the lively wit of its editor, George D. Prentice, and for this newspaper he paid regularly when he had not the means to buy decent clothing. From this time his life rapidly increases in interest. It is certain that, from early youth, he had quietly determined to become great, and that he thoroughly tested his own talents and acquirements before entering upon politics as a career. His chief and indeed his almost only talent was resolute perseverance, and by means of it he passed in the race of life thousands who were his superiors in genius. Among all the biographies of the great and wise and good among mankind, there is not one so full of encouragement to poor young men as that of Abraham Lincoln, since there is not one which so illustrates not only how mere personal success may be attained, but how, by strong will and self-culture, the tremendous task of guiding a vast country through the trials of a civil war may be successfully achieved.

In the spring of 1832, Mr. Offutt failed, and Lincoln had nothing to do. For some time past, an Indian rebellion, led by the famous Black Hawk, Chief of the Sac tribe, had caused the greatest alarm in the Western States. About the beginning of this century (1804-5), the Sacs had been removed west of the Mississippi; but Black Hawk, believing that his people had been unjustly exiled, organised a conspiracy which for a while embraced nine of the most powerful tribes of the North-West, and announced his intention of returning and settling in the old hunting-grounds of his people on the Rock River. He was a man of great courage and shrewdness, skilled as an orator, and dreaded as one gifted with supernatural power, combining in his person the war-chief and prophet. But the returning Indians, by committing great barbarities on the way, caused such irritation and alarm among the white settlers, that when Governor Reynolds, of Illinois, issued a call for volunteers, several regiments of hardy frontiersmen were at once formed. Black Hawk's allies, with the exception of the tribe of the Foxes, at once fell away, but their desperate leader kept on in his course. Among the companies which volunteered was one from Menard County, embracing many men from New Salem. The captain was chosen by vote, and the choice fell on Lincoln. He was accustomed to say, when President, that nothing in his life had ever gratified him so much as this promotion; and this may well have been, since, to a very ambitious man, the first practical proofs of popularity are like the first instalment of a great fortune paid to one who is poor.

Though he was never in an actual engagement during this campaign, Lincoln underwent much hunger and hardship while it lasted, and at times had great trouble with his men, who were not only mere raw militia, but also unusually rough and rebellious. One incident of the war, however, as narrated by Lamon, not only indicates that Abraham Lincoln was sometimes in danger, but was well qualified to grapple with it.

"One day, during these many marches and countermarches, an old Indian, weary, hungry, and helpless, found his way into the camp. He professed to be a friend of the whites; and, although it was an exceedingly perilous experiment for one of his colour, he ventured to throw himself upon the mercy of the soldiers. But the men first murmured, and then broke out into fierce cries for his blood. "We have come out to fight Indians," they said, "and we intend to do it." The poor Indian, now in the extremity of his distress and peril, did what he should have done before—he threw down before his assailants a soiled and crumpled paper, which he implored them to read before taking his life. It was a letter of character and safe conduct from General Cass, pronouncing him a faithful man, who had done good service in the cause for which this army was enlisted. But it was too late; the men refused to read it, or thought it a forgery, and were rushing with fury upon the defenceless old savage, when Captain Lincoln bounded between them and their appointed victim. "Men," said he, and his voice for a moment stilled the agitation around him, "this must not be done—he must not be shot and killed by us." "But," said some of them, "the Indian is a spy." Lincoln knew that his own life was now in only less danger than that of the poor creature that crouched behind him. During this scene, the towering form and the passion and resolution in Lincoln's face produced an effect upon the furious mob. They paused, listened, fell back, and then sullenly obeyed what seemed to be the voice of reason as well as authority. But there were still some murmurs of disappointed rage, and half-suppressed exclamations which looked towards vengeance of some kind. At length one of the men, a little bolder than the rest, but evidently feeling that he spoke for the whole, cried out— "This is cowardly on your part, Lincoln!" "If any man think I am a coward, let him test it," was the reply. "Lincoln," responded a new voice, "you are larger and heavier than we are." "This you can guard against; choose your weapons," returned the Captain. Whatever may be said of Mr. Lincoln's choice of means for the preservation of military discipline, it was certainly very effectual in this case. There was no more disaffection in his camp, and the word "coward" was never coupled with his name again. Mr. Lincoln understood his men better than those who would be disposed to criticise his conduct. He has often declared himself that "his life and character were both at stake, and would probably have been lost, had he not at that supremely critical moment forgotten the officer and asserted the man." The soldiers, in fact, could not have been arrested, tried, or punished; they were merely wild backwoodsmen, "acting entirely by their own will, and any effort to court-martial them would simply have failed in its object, and made their Captain seem afraid of them."

During this campaign, Lincoln made the acquaintance of a lawyer—then captain—the Hon. T. Stuart, who had subsequently a great influence on his career. When the company was mustered out in May, Lincoln at once re-enlisted as a private in a volunteer spy company, where he remained for a month, until the Battle of Bad Axe, which resulted in the capture of Black Hawk, put an end to hostilities. This war was not a remarkable affair, says J. G. Holland, but it was remarkable that the two simplest, homeliest, and truest men engaged in it afterwards became Presidents of the United States—namely, General, then Colonel, Zachary Taylor and Abraham Lincoln.

It has always been usual in the United States to urge to the utmost the slightest military services rendered by candidates for office. The absurd degree to which this was carried often awoke the satire of Lincoln, even when it was at his own expense. Many years after, he referred thus humorously to his military services[1]:—

---

[1] Raymond, "Life and Public Services of Abraham Lincoln," p. 25.

"By the way, Mr. Speaker, did you know I was a military hero? Yes, sir, in the days of the Black Hawk war I fought, bled, and came away. Speaking of General Cass's career reminds me of my own. I was not at Sullivan's defeat, but I was about as near to it as Cass was to Hull's surrender, and, like him, I saw the place soon after. It is quite certain that I did not break my sword, for I had none to break;[1] but I bent my musket pretty badly on one occasion. If Cass broke his sword, the idea is he broke it in desperation. I bent the musket by accident. If General Cass went in advance of me in picking whortleberries, I guess I surpassed him in charges upon the wild onions. If he saw any live fighting Indians, it was more than I did; but I had a great many bloody struggles with the mosquitoes, and, although I never fainted from loss of blood, I certainly can say I was often very hungry."

The soldiers from Sangamon County arrived home just ten days before the State election, and Lincoln was immediately applied to for permission to place

---

[1] Mr. Lincoln "spoke forgetfully" on this occasion. Owing to the drunkenness and insubordination of his men, which he could not help, he was once obliged to carry a wooden sword for two days.—Lamon, p. 104. On a previous occasion, he had been under arrest, and was deprived of *his sword* for one day, for firing a pistol within ten steps of camp.—*Ibid.*, p. 103.

his name among the candidates for the Legislature.[1] He canvassed the district, but was defeated, though he received the almost unanimous vote of his own precinct. The young man had, however, made a great advance even by defeat, since he became known by it as one whose sterling honesty had deserved a better reward. Lincoln's integrity was, in this election, strikingly evinced by his adherence to his political principles; had he been less scrupulous, he would not have lost the election. At this time there were two great political parties—the Democratic, headed by Andrew Jackson, elected President in 1832, and that which had been the Federalist, but which was rapidly being called Whig. The Democratic party warred against a national bank, paper money, "monopolies" or privileged and chartered institutions, a protective tariff, and internal improvements, and was, in short, jealous of all public expenditure which could tend to greatly enrich individuals. Its leader, Jackson, was a man of inflexible determination and unquestionable bravery, which he had shown not only in battle, but by subduing the incipient rebellion in South Carolina, when that state had threatened to nullify or secede from the Union. Lincoln's heart was with Jackson; he had unbounded admiration for the man, but he

---

[1] Holland, p. 53.

knew that the country needed internal improvements, and in matters of political economy inclined to the Whigs.

After returning from the army, he went to live in the house of W. H. Herndon, a most estimable man, to whose researches the world owes nearly all that is known of Lincoln's early life and family, and who was subsequently his law-partner. At this time the late Captain thought of becoming a blacksmith, but as an opportunity occurred of buying a store in New Salem on credit, he became, in company with a man named Berry, a country merchant, or trader.

He showed little wisdom in associating himself with Berry, who proved a drunkard, and ruined the business, after a year of anxiety, leaving Lincoln in debt, which he struggled to pay off through many years of trouble. It was not until 1849 that the last note was discharged. His creditors were, however, considerate and kind. While living with Mr. Herndon, Lincoln began to study law seriously. He had previously read Blackstone, and by one who has really mastered this grand compendium of English law the profession is already half-acquired. He was still very poor, and appears to have lived by helping a Mr. Ellis in his shop, and to have received much willing aid from friends, especially John T. Stuart, who always cheerfully supplied his wants, and lent him law-books.

About this time, Lincoln attracted the attention of a noted Democrat, John Calhoun, the surveyor of Sangamon County, who afterwards became famous as President of the Lecompton Council in Kansas, during the disturbances between the friends and opponents of slavery prior to the admission of the state. He liked Lincoln, and, wanting a really honest assistant, recommended him to learn surveying, lending him a book for the purpose. In six weeks he had qualified himself, and soon acquired a small private business.

On the 7th May, 1833, Lincoln was appointed postmaster at New Salem. As the mail arrived but once a-week, neither the duties nor emoluments of the office were such as to greatly disturb or delight him. He is said, indeed, to have kept the letters in his hat, being at once, in his own person, both office and officer. The advantages which he gained were opportunities to read the newspapers, which he did aloud to the assembled inhabitants, and to decipher letters for all who could not read. All of this was conducive, in a creditable way, to notoriety and popularity, and he improved it as such. In the autumn of 1834, a great trouble occurred. His scanty property, consisting of the horse, saddle, bridle, and surveyor's instruments by which he lived, were seized under a judgment on one of the notes which he had given for "the store." But two good friends, named Short and Bowlin Greene, bought them in for 245 dollars, which Lincoln faithfully repaid in due time. It is said that he was an accurate surveyor, and remarkable for his truthfulness. He never speculated in lands, nor availed himself of endless opportunities to profit, by aiding the speculations of others.

Miserably poor and badly clad, Lincoln, though very fond of the society of women, was sensitive and shy when they were strangers. Mr. Ellis, the storekeeper for whom he often worked, states that, when he lived with him at the tavern, there came a lady from Virginia with three stylish daughters, who remained a few weeks. "During their stay, I do not remember Mr. Lincoln ever eating at the same table where they did. I thought it was on account of his awkward appearance and wearing apparel." There are many anecdotes recorded of this kind, showing at this period his poverty, his popularity, and his kindness of heart. He was referee, umpire, and unquestioned judge in all disputes, horse-races, or wagers. One who knew him in this capacity said of him—"He is the fairest man I ever had to deal with."

In 1834, Lincoln again became a successful candidate for the Legislature of Illinois, receiving a larger majority than any other candidate on the ticket. A friend, Colonel Smoot, lent him 200 dollars to make a decent appearance, and he went to the seat of government properly dressed, for, perhaps, the first time in his life. During the session, he said very little, but worked hard and learned much. He was on the Committee for Public Accounts and Expenditures, and when the session was at an end, quietly walked back to his work.

Lamon relates, at full length, that at this time Lincoln was in love with a young lady, who died of a broken heart in 1835, not, however, for Lincoln, but for another young man who had been engaged to, and abandoned her. At her death, Lincoln seemed for some weeks nearly insane, and was never the same man again. From this time he lost his youth, and became subject to frequent attacks of intense mental depression, resulting in that settled melancholy which never left him.

In 1836, he was again elected to the Legislature. Political excitement at this time ran high. The country was being settled rapidly, and people's minds were wild with speculation in lands and public works, from which every man hoped for wealth, and which were to be developed by the legislators. Lincoln's colleagues were in an unusual degree able men, and the session was a busy one. It was during the canvass of 1836 that he made his first really great speech. He had by this time fairly joined the new

Whig party, and it was in reply to a Democrat, Dr. Early, that he spoke. From that day he was recognised as one of the most powerful orators in the state.

The principal object of this session, in accordance with the popular mania, was internal improvements, and to this subject Lincoln had been devoted for years. The representatives from Sangamon County consisted of nine men of great influence, every one at least six feet in height, whence they were known as the Long Nine. The friends of the adoption of a general system of internal improvements wished to secure the aid of the Long Nine, but the latter refused to aid them unless the removal of the capital of the state from Vandalia to Springfield should be made a part of the measure. The result was that both the Bill for removal and that for internal improvements, involving the indebtedness of the state for many millions of dollars, passed the same day. Lincoln was the leader in these improvements, and "was a most laborious member, instant in season and out of season for the great measures of the Whig party."[1] At the present day, though grave doubts

---

[1] Holland passes over the wisdom or unwisdom of these measures without comment. According to Ford ("History of Illinois") and Lamon, the whole state was by them "simply bought up and bribed to support the most senseless and disastrous policy which ever crippled the energies of a growing country." It is certain that, in any country where the internal resources are enormous and the inhabitants intelligent, enterprising, and poor, such legislation will always find favour.

may exist as to the expediency of such reckless and radical legislation, there can be none as to the integrity or good faith of Abraham Lincoln. He did not enrich himself by it, though it is not impossible that, in legislation as in land-surveying, others swindled on his honesty.

It was during this session that Lincoln first beheld Stephen Douglas, who was destined to become, for twenty years, his most formidable opponent. Douglas, from his diminutive stature and great mind, was afterwards popularly known as the Little Giant. Lincoln merely recorded his first impressions of Douglas by saying he was the least man he ever saw. This legislation of 1836-37 was indeed of a nature to attract speculators, whether in finance or politics. Within a few days, it passed two loans amounting to 12,000,000 dollars, and chartered 1,300 miles of railway, with canals, bridges, and river improvements in full proportion. The capital stock of two banks was increased by nearly 5,000,000 dollars, which the State took, leaving it to the banks to manage the railroad and canal funds. Everything was undertaken on a colossal and daring scale by the legislators, who were principally managed by the Long Nine, who were in their turn chiefly directed by Lincoln. The previous session had been to him only as the green-room in which to prepare himself for the stage. When he made this his first appearance in the political *ballet*, it was certainly with such a leap as had never before been witnessed in any beginner. The internal improvement scheme involved not only great boldness and promptness in its execution, but also a vast amount of that practical business talent in which most "Western men" and Yankees are instinctively proficient. With all this, there was incessant hard work and great excitement. Through the turmoil, Lincoln passed like one in his true element. He had at last got into the life to which he had aspired for years, and was probably as happy as his constitutional infirmity of melancholy would permit. He was, it is true, no man of business in the ordinary sense, but he understood the general principles of business, and was skilled in availing himself in others of talents which he did not possess.

During this session, he put on record his first anti-slavery protest. It was, in the words of Lamon, "a very mild beginning," but it required uncommon courage, and is interesting as indicating the principle upon which his theory of Emancipation was afterwards carried out. At this time the whole country, North as well as South, was becoming excited concerning the doctrines and practices of the small but very rapidly-growing body of Abolitionists, who were attacking slavery with fiery zeal, and provoking in return the most deadly hatred. The Abolitionist, carrying the Republican theory to its logical extreme, insisted that all men, white or black, were entitled to the same political and social rights; the slave-owners honestly believed that society should consist of strata, the lowest of which should be bondmen. The Abolitionist did not recognise that slavery in America, like serfdom in Russia, had developed into culture a country which would, without it, have remained a wilderness; nor did the slave theorists recognise that a time must infallibly come when both systems of enforced labour must yield to new forms of industrial development. The Abolitionists, taking their impressions from the early English and Quaker philanthropists, thought principally of the personal wrong inflicted on the negro; while the majority of Americans declared, with equal conviction, that the black's sufferings were not of so much account that white men should be made to suffer much more for them, and the whole country be possibly overwhelmed in civil war. Even at this early period of the dispute, there were, however, in the old Whig party, a few men who thought that the growing strife was not to be stopped simply by crushing the Abolitionists. But while they would gladly have seen the latter abate their furious zeal, they also thought that slavery might, with propriety, be at least checked in its progress, since they had observed, with grave misgiving, that wherever it was planted, only an aristocracy flourished, while the poor white men became utterly degraded. Such were the views of Abraham Lincoln—views which, in after years, led, during the sharp and bitter need of the war, to the formation of the theory of Emancipation for the sake of the Country, as opposed to mere Abolition for the sake of the Negro, which had had its turn and fulfilled its mission.

The feeling against the Abolitionists was very bitter in Illinois. Many other states had passed severe resolutions, recommending that anti-slavery agitation be made an indictable offence, or a misdemeanour; and in May, 1836, Congress declared that all future "abolition petitions" should be laid on the table without discussion. But when the Legislature of Illinois took its turn in the fashion, and passed resolutions of the same kind, Abraham Lincoln presented to the House a protest which he could get but one man, Dan Stone, to sign. Perhaps he did not want any more signatures, for he was one of those who foresaw to what this cloud, no larger than a man's hand, would in future years extend, and was willing to be alone as a prophet. The protest was as follows:—

March 3, 1837.

The following protest was presented to the House, which was read and ordered to be spread on the journals, to wit:—

Resolutions upon the subject of domestic slavery having

passed both branches of the General Assembly at its present session, the undersigned hereby protest against the passage of the same.

They believe that the institution of slavery is founded on both injustice and bad policy; but that the promulgation of Abolition doctrines tends rather to increase than abate its evils.

They believe that the Congress of the United States has no power under the Constitution to interfere with the institution of slavery in the different states.

They believe that the Congress of the United States has the power, under the Constitution, to abolish slavery in the district of Columbia; but that the power ought not to be exercised, unless at the request of the people of the district.

The difference between these opinions and those contained in the said resolutions is their reason for entering this protest.

     (Signed) DAN STONE.
           A. LINCOLN.
Representatives from the County of Sangamon.

This was indeed a very mild protest, but it was the beginning of that which, in after years, grew to be the real Emancipation of the negro. Never in history was so fine an end of the wedge succeeded by such a wide cleaving bulk. Much as Lincoln afterwards accomplished for the abolition of slavery, he never, says Holland, became more extreme in his views than the words of this protest intimate. It was during this session also that he first put himself in direct opposition to Douglas by another protest. The Democrats, in order to enable the *aliens*—virtually the Irishmen—in their state to vote on six months' residence, passed a Bill known as the Douglas Bill, remodelling the judiciary in such a way as to secure judges who would aid them. Against this, Lincoln, E. D. Baker, and others protested vigorously, but without avail. Both of these protests, though failures at the time, were in reality the beginnings of the two great principles which led to Lincoln's great success, and the realisation of his utmost ambition. During his life, defeat was always a step to victory.

CHAPTER III.

Lincoln settles at Springfield as a Lawyer—Candidate for the Office of Presidential Elector—A Love Affair—Marries Miss Todd—Religious Views—Exerts himself for Henry Clay—Elected to Congress in 1846—Speeches in Congress—Out of Political Employment until 1854—Anecdotes of Lincoln as a Lawyer.

ABRAHAM LINCOLN'S career was now clear. He was to follow the law for a living, as a step to political eminence. And as the seat of State Government was henceforth to be at Springfield, he determined to live where both law and politics might be followed to the greatest advantage, since it was in Springfield that, in addition to the State Courts, the Circuit and District Courts of the United States sat. He obtained his license as an attorney in 1837, and commenced his practice in the March of that year. He entered into partnership with his friend, J. T. Stewart, and lived with the Hon. W. Butler, who was of great assistance to him in the simple matter of living, for he was at this time as poor as ever. During 1837, he delivered several addresses, in which there was a strong basis of common sense, though they were fervid and figurative to extravagance, as suited the tastes of his hearers. In these speeches he predicted the great struggle on which the country was about to enter, and that it would never be settled by passion but by reason—"cold, calculating, unimpassioned reasoning, which must furnish all the materials for our future defence and support." He also distinguished himself in debate and retort, so that ere long he became unrivalled, in his sphere, in ready eloquence. From this time, for twenty years, he followed his great political rival, Douglas, seeking every opportunity to contend with him. From 1837 he concerned himself little with the politics of his state, but entered with zeal into the higher interests of the Federal Union.

In 1840, Lincoln was a candidate for the office of Presidential elector on the Harrison ticket, and made speeches through a great part of Illinois. Soon after, he again became involved in a love affair, which, through its perplexities and the revival of the memory of his early disappointment, had a terrible effect upon his mind. He had become intimate with a Mr. Speed, who remained through life his best friend. For a year he was almost a lunatic, and was taken to Kentucky by Mr. Speed, and kept there until he recovered. It was for this reason that he did not attend the Legislature of 1841–42. It is very characteristic of Lincoln that, from boyhood, he never wanted true friends to aid him in all his troubles.

Soon after his recovery, Lincoln became engaged

to Miss Mary Todd. This lady was supposed to be gifted as a witty and satirical writer, though it must be admitted that the specimens of her literary capacity, exhibited in certain anonymous contributions to the newspapers, show little talent beyond the art of irritation. Several of these were levelled at a politician named James Shields, an Irishman, who, being told that Lincoln had written them, sent him a challenge. The challenge was accepted, but the duel was prevented by mutual friends. Lincoln married Miss Todd on the 4th November, 1842. This marriage, which had not been preceded by the most favourable omens, was followed by a singular misfortune. In 1843, Lincoln was a Whig candidate for Congress, but was defeated. "He had a hard time of it, and was compelled to meet accusations of a strange character. Among other things, he was charged with being an aristocrat, and with having deserted his old friends, the people, by marrying a proud woman on account of her blood and family. This hurt him keenly," says Lamon, "and he took great pains to disprove it." Other accusations, equally frivolous, relative to his supposed religion or irreligion, also contributed to his defeat.

On this much-vexed subject of Lincoln's religious faith, or his want of it, something may here be said. In his boyhood, when religious associations are most valuable in disciplining the mind, he had never even seen a church, and, as he grew older, his sense of humour and his rude companions prevented him from being seriously impressed by the fervid but often eccentric oratory of the few itinerant preachers who found their way into the backwoods. At New Salem, he had read "Volney's Ruins" and the works of Thomas Paine, and was for some time a would-be unbeliever. It is easy to trace in his youthful irreligion the influence of irresistible causes. As he grew older, his intensely melancholy and emotional temperament inclined him towards reliance in an unseen Providence and belief in a future state; and it is certain that, after the unpopularity of free-thinkers had forced itself upon his mind, the most fervidly passionate expressions of piety began to abound in his speeches. In this he was not, however, hypocritical. From his childhood, Abraham Lincoln was possessed even to unreason with the idea that whatever was absolutely popular, was founded on reason and right. He was a Republican of Republicans, faithfully believing that whatever average common sense accepted must be followed.[1] His own personal popularity was at all times very great.

---

[1] His biographies abound in proof of this. "He believed that a man, in order to effect anything, should work through organisations of men."—Holland, p. 92. It is very difficult for any one not brought up in the United States to realise the degree to which this idea can influence men, and determine their whole moral nature.

One who knew him testifies that, when the lawyers travelling the judicial circuit of Illinois arrived at the villages where trials were to be held, crowds of men and women always assembled to welcome Abraham Lincoln.

Lincoln himself had a great admiration for Henry Clay. In 1844, he went through Illinois delivering speeches and debating and speaking, or, as it is called in America, "stumping" for him, and he even extended his labours into Indiana. It was all in vain, and Clay's defeat was a great blow to Lincoln.[1] At this time, though he withdrew from politics in favour of law, he began to think seriously of getting a seat in Congress. His management of this affair indicates forcibly his entire faith in party-right, and his principle of *never* advancing beyond his party. Of all the men of action known to history as illustrating great epochs, there never was a more thorough man of action than Lincoln, but the brain which inspired his action was always that of the people.

Through all his poverty, Lincoln was always just and generous. In 1843, while living with his wife for four dollars a-week, at a country tavern, he gave up a promissory-note for a large fee to an impoverished client who, after the trial, had lost a hand.

---

[1] It is a matter of regret that, when Lincoln, long after, went to see his idol and ideal, he was greatly disappointed in him.—Holland, p. 95. Lamon denies this visit, but does not disprove it.

He paid all his own debts, and generously aided his stepmother and other friends.

In 1846, Lincoln accepted the nomination for Congress. His Democratic opponent was Peter Cartwright, a celebrated pioneer Methodist preacher. It is a great proof of Lincoln's popularity that he was elected by an unprecedented majority, though he was the only Whig Congressman from Illinois. At this session, his almost life-long adversary, Douglas, took a place in the Senate. Both houses shone with an array of great and brilliant names, and Lincoln, as the only representative of his party from his state, was in a critical and responsible situation. But he was no novice in legislation, and he acquitted himself bravely. He became a member of the Committee on Post Offices and Post Roads, and in that capacity made his first speech. He found it as easy a matter to address his new colleagues as his old clients. "I was about as badly scared," he wrote to W. J. Herndon, "and no worse, as when I speak in court." During this session, the United States were at war with Mexico, and Lincoln was, with his party, in a painful dilemma. They were opposed to the principle of the war, since they detested forcible acquisition of territory, and it was evident that Mexico was wanted by the South to extend the area of slavery. Yet they could not, in humanity, withhold supplies from the army in Mexico while fighting bravely.

So Lincoln denounced the war, and yet voted the supplies—an inconsistency creditable to his heart, but which involved him in trouble with his constituents. But he struck the Administration a severe blow in what was really his first speech before the whole House. President Polk having declared, in a Message, that "the Mexicans had invaded our territory, and shed the blood of our citizens on our own soil," Lincoln introduced what were called the famous "spot resolutions," in which the President was invited in a series of satirical yet serious questions to indicate the spot where this outrage had been committed.

Lincoln was very busy this year. The Whig National Convention was to nominate a candidate for President on the 1st June, and he was to be one of its members. On July 27th, he delivered, in Congress, a speech as remarkable in some respects for solid sense and shrewdness as it was in others for eccentric drollery and scathing Western retorts. The second session, 1848–49, was quieter. At one time he proposed, as a substitute for a resolution that slavery be at once abolished by law in the district of Columbia, another, providing that the owners be paid for their slaves. If he did little in this session to attract attention, he made for himself a name, and was known as a powerful speaker and a rising man; but, after returning to Springfield, though a Whig President had been elected, and his own reputation greatly increased, he was thrown out of political employment until the year 1854. He made great efforts to secure the office of Commissioner of the General Land Office, but failed. President Fillmore, it is true, offered him the Governorship of Oregon, but Mrs. Lincoln induced him to decline it.

In 1850, his friends wished to nominate him for Congress, but he positively refused the honour. It is thought that he wished to establish himself in his profession for the sake of a support for his family, or that he had entered into a secret understanding with other candidates for Congress, who were to nominally oppose each other, but in reality secure election in turn by excluding rivals.[1] But it is most probable that he clearly foresaw at this time the tremendous struggle which was approaching between North and South, and wished to prepare himself for some great part in it. To engage in minor political battles and be defeated, as would probably be the case in his district, where his war-vote in Congress was still remembered to his disadvantage, would have

---

[1] Lamon, p. 275, says there can be no doubt that Mr. Lincoln *would* have cheerfully made such a dishonourable and tricky agreement, but inclines to think he did not. It is very doubtful whether the compact, if it existed at all, was not made simply for the purpose of excluding the Democrats.

seriously injured his future prospects of every kind. He said, in 1850, to his friend Stuart—"The time will come when we must all be Democrats or Abolitionists. When that time comes, my mind is made up. The slavery question can't be compromised."

Many interesting anecdotes of Lincoln's legal experiences at this time have been preserved. In his first case, at Springfield, he simply admitted that all laws and precedents were in favour of his opponent, and, having stated them in detail, left the decision to the Court. He would never take an unjust, or mean, or a purely litigious case. When retained with a colleague, named Swett, to defend a man accused of murder, Lincoln became convinced of his client's guilt, and said to his associate—"You must defend him—I cannot." Mr. Swett obtained an acquittal, but Lincoln would take no part of the large fee which was paid. On one occasion, however, when one of his own friends of boyhood, John Armstrong, was indicted for a very atrocious murder, Lincoln, moved by the tears and entreaties of the aged mother of the prisoner, consented to plead his cause. It having been testified that, when the man was murdered, the full moon was shining high in the heavens, Lincoln, producing an almanac, proved that, on the night in question, there was in fact no moon at all. Those who were associated with him for years declare that they never knew a lawyer who was so moderate in his charges. Though he attained great reputation in his profession, the highest fee he ever received was 5,000 dollars. His strength lay entirely in shrewd common sense, in quickly mastering all the details of a case, and in ready eloquence or debate, for he had very little law-learning, and was averse to making researches. But his rare genius for promptly penetrating all the difficulties of a legal or political problem, which aided him so much as President, enabled him to deal with juries in a masterly manner. On one occasion, when thirty-four witnesses swore to a fact on one side, and exactly as many on the other, Mr. Lincoln proposed a very practical test to the jury—"If you were going to *bet* on this case," he said, "on which side would you lay a picayune?"[1]

Any poor person in distress for want of legal aid could always find a zealous friend in Lincoln. On one occasion, a poor old negro woman came to him and Mr. Herndon, complaining that her son had been imprisoned at New Orleans for simply going, in his ignorance, ashore, thereby breaking a disgraceful law which then existed, forbidding free men of colour from other states to enter Louisiana. Having been condemned to pay a fine, and being without

---

[1] Holland, p. 82. A picayune is six cents, or 3d.

money, the poor man was about to be sold for a slave. Messrs. Lincoln and Herndon, finding law of no avail, ransomed the prisoner out of their own pockets. In those days, a free-born native of a Northern state could, if of African descent, be seized and sold simply for setting foot on Southern soil.

CHAPTER IV.

Rise of the Southern Party—Formation of the Abolition and the Free Soil Parties—Judge Douglas and the Kansas-Nebraska Bill—Douglas defeated by Lincoln—Lincoln resigns as Candidate for Congress—Lincoln's Letter on Slavery—The Bloomington Speech—The Fremont Campaign—Election of Buchanan—The Dred-Scott Decision.

THE great storm of civil war which now threatened the American Ship of State had been long brewing. Year by year the party of slave-owners—small in number but strong in union, and unanimously devoted to the acquisition of political power—had progressed, until they saw before them the possibility of ruling the entire continent. To please them, the nation, after purchasing, had admitted as slave territory the immense regions of Louisiana and Florida, and in their interests a war had been waged with Mexico. But, so early as 1820, the North, alarmed at the incredible progress of slave-power, and observing that wherever it was established white labour was paralysed, and that society resolved itself at once into a small aristocracy, with a large number of blacks and poor whites who were systematically degraded,[1] attempted to check its territorial

---

[1] There were no free schools in South Carolina until 1852, and it was a serious crime to teach a negro to read.

extension. There was a contest, which was finally settled by what was known as the Missouri Compromise, by which it was agreed that Missouri should be admitted as a slave state, but that in future all territory North and West of Missouri, above latitude 36° 30′, should be for ever free.[1]

While the inhabitants of the Eastern and Western States applied themselves to every development of industrial pursuits, art, and letters, the Southerners lived by agricultural slave-labour, and were entirely devoted to acquiring political power. The contest was unequal, and the result was that, before the Rebellion, the slave-holders—who, with their slaves, only constituted one-third of the population of the United States—had secured *two*-thirds of all the offices—civil, military, or naval—and had elected two-thirds of the Presidents. Law after law was passed, giving the slave-holders every advantage, until Governor Henry A. Wise, of Virginia, declared in Congress that slavery should pour itself abroad, and have no limit but the Southern Ocean. He also asserted that the best way to meet or answer Abolition arguments was *with death*. His house was afterwards, during the war, used for a negro school, under care of a New England Abolitionist. Large pecuniary rewards were offered by Governors of slave states for the persons—*i.e.*, the lives—of eminent Northern anti-slavery men. Direct

---

[1] Arnold, "History of Lincoln," p. 33.

efforts were made to re-establish the slave-trade between Africa and the Southern States.

In 1839 the Abolition party was formed, which advocated the total abolition of slavery. This was going too far for the mass of the North, who hoped to live at peace with the South. But still there were many in both the Whig and Democratic parties who wished to see the advance of the slave power checked; and their delegates, meeting at Buffalo in June, 1848, formed the Free Soil party, opposed to the further extension of slavery, which rapidly grew in power. The struggle became violent. When the territory acquired by war from Mexico was to be admitted to the Union in 1846, David Wilmot, of Pennsylvania, offered a proviso to the Bill accepting the territory, to the effect that slavery should be unknown in it. There was a fierce debate for two years over this proviso, which was finally rejected. The most desperate legislation was adopted to make California a slave state, and when she decided by her own will to be free, the slave-holders opposed her admission to the Union. Finally, in 1850, the celebrated Compromise Measures were adopted. These were to the effect that California should be admitted free—that in New Mexico and Utah the people should decide for themselves as to slavery—and that such of Texas as was above latitude 36° 30′ should be free. To this, however, was tacked a new and more cruel fugitive slave law,[1] apparently to humiliate and annoy the free states, and to keep irritation alive.

But, on the 4th January, 1854, Judge Douglas introduced into the Senate of the United States a Bill known as the Kansas-Nebraska Bill, proposing to set aside the Missouri Compromise. This was passed, after a tremendous struggle, on May 22nd, and the slave-party triumphed. Yet it proved their ruin, for it was the first decisive step to the strife which ended in civil war. It eventually destroyed Mr. Douglas, its originator. He is said to have repented the deed; and when it became evident that the Union was aroused, and that the Republican

---

[1] A law by which slaves who had escaped to free states were returned to their owners. The writer, as a boy, has seen many cruel instances of the manner in which the old slave law was carried out. But while great pains were taken to hunt down and return slaves who had escaped to free states, there was literally nothing done to return free coloured people who had been inveigled or carried by force to the South, and there sold as slaves. It was believed that, at one time, hardly a day passed during which a free black was not thus entrapped from Pennsylvania. The writer once knew, in Philadelphia, a boy of purely white blood, but of dark complexion, who narrowly escaped being kidnapped by downright violence, that he might be "sent South." White children were commonly terrified by parents or nurses with "the kidnappers," who would black their faces, and sell them. Even in the Northern cities, there were few grown-up negro men who had not, at one time or another, been hunted by the lower classes of whites through the streets in the most incredibly barbarous manner.

would be the winning party, Douglas went over to it. "He had long before invoked destruction on the ruthless hand which should disturb the compromise, and now he put forth his own ingenious hand to do the deed and to take the curse, in both of which he was eminently successful." He was defeated by the honester and wiser Lincoln, and died a disappointed man.

To suit the slave-party, it was originally agreed, in 1820, that in future they, though so greatly inferior in number, should have half the territory of the Union. But as they found in time that population increased most rapidly in the free territories, the compromise of 1850 was arranged, by which the inhabitants of the new states were to decide for themselves in the matter. The result was an immediate and terrible turmoil. The legitimate dwellers in Kansas were almost all steady, law-abiding farmers who hated slavery. But, from Missouri and the neighbouring slave states, there was poured in, by means of committees and funds raised in the South, a vast number of "Border ruffians," or desperadoes, who would remain in Kansas only long enough to vote illegally, or to rob and ravage, and then retire. The North, on the other hand, exasperated by these outrages, sent numbers of emigrants to Kansas to support the legitimate settlers, and the result was a virtual civil war, which was the more irritating because

President Buchanan did all in his power to aid the Border ruffians, and crush the legitimate settlers. Day by day it became evident that the Kansas-Nebraska Bill had been passed for the purpose of enabling the South to quit the Union, and ere long this was openly avowed by the slave-holding press and politicians. The entire North was now fiercely irritated. Judge Douglas, returning westwards, tried to speak at Chicago, but was hissed down. At the state fair in Springfield, Illinois, Oct. 4th, 1854, he spoke in defence of the Nebraska Bill, but was replied to by Lincoln "with such power as he had never exhibited before." He was no longer the orator he had been, "but a newer and greater Lincoln, the like of whom no one in that vast multitude had ever heard." "The Nebraska Bill," says W. H. Herndon, "was shivered, and, like a tree of the forest, was torn and rent asunder by hot bolts of truth." Douglas was crushed, and his brief reply was a spiritless failure. From this time forth, Lincoln's speeches were as unexceptional in form as they were vigorous and logical. Never was there a man of whom it could be said with so much truth that he always rose to the occasion, however great, however unprecedented its demands on his power might be.

From Springfield Lincoln followed Douglas to Peoria, where he delivered, in debate, another great speech. Not liking slavery in itself, Lincoln was willing to let it alone under the old compromise, but he would never suffer its introduction to new territories, and he made it clear as day that Douglas, by opening the flood-gate of slavery on free soil, had let loose a torrent which, if unchecked, would sweep everything to destruction. He had previously, at Springfield, disclosed the fallacy of Douglas's "great principle" by a single sentence. "I admit that the emigrant to Kansas is competent to govern himself, but I deny his right to govern any other person without that person's consent." Such arguments were overwhelming, and Douglas, the Giant of the West and the foremost politician in America, felt that he had met his master at his own peculiar weapons—oratory and debate. He sent for Lincoln, and proposed that both should refrain from speaking during the campaign, and Lincoln, conscious of superior strength, agreed. Douglas did speak once more, however, but Lincoln remained silent.

At the end of this campaign, Lincoln was elected to the Legislature of Illinois. As the Legislature was about to elect a United States Senator, Lincoln resigned to become a candidate. But at the election —there being three candidates—Lincoln, finding that by resigning he could make it sure that an *anti-*Nebraska man (Judge Trumbull) could be elected, and that there was some uncertainty as to his own success, resigned, in the noblest manner, in favour of his principles and party. It had been the ambition of his life to become a United States Senator. The result of this sacrifice, says Holland, was that, when the Republican party was soon after regularly organised, Lincoln became their foremost man.

Meanwhile, the strife in Kansas grew more desperate. One Governor after another was appointed to the state, for the express purpose of turning it over to slavery; but the outrageous frauds practised at the election were too much for Mr. Reeder and his successor, Shannon, and even for his follower, Robert J. Walker, a man not over-scrupulous. Walker, like many other Democrats, adroitly turned with the tide; but too late.

During 1855, the old parties were breaking up, and the new Republican one was gathering with great rapidity. Two separate governments or legislatures had formed in Kansas, one manifestly and boldly fraudulent in favour of slavery, and the other settled at Topeka, headed by Governor Reeder, consisting of legitimate settlers. At this time, Aug. 24th, 1855, Lincoln wrote to his friend Speed a letter, in which he discussed slavery with great shrewdness. In answer to the standing Southern argument, that slavery did not concern Northern people, and that it was none of their business, he replied—

"In 1841, you and I had together a tedious low-water trip on a steamboat, from Louisville to St. Louis. You may remember as well as I do that, from Louisville to the mouth of the Ohio, there were on board ten or a dozen slaves shackled with irons. That sight was a continual torment to me, and I see something like it every time I touch the Ohio, or any other slave-border. It is not fair for you to assume that I have no interest in a thing which has, and continually exercises, the power of making me miserable. You ought rather to appreciate how much the great body of the Northern people do crucify their feelings, in order to maintain their loyalty to the Constitution and the Union. I do oppose the extension of slavery, because my judgment and feelings so prompt me; and I am under no obligations to the contrary. If for this you and I must differ, differ we must."

On May 29th, 1856, Lincoln attended a meeting at Bloomington, Illinois, where, with his powerful assistance, the Republican party of the state was organised, and delegates were appointed to the National Republican Convention which was to be held on the 17th of the following month at Philadelphia. The speech which he made on this occasion was of extraordinary power. From this day he was regarded by the Republicans of the West as their leader. Therefore, in the Republican National Convention of 1856, at Philadelphia, the Illinois delegation presented his name for the Vice-Presidency. He received a complimentary vote of 110 votes, the successful candidate, Dayton, having 259. This, however, was his formal introduction to the nation. At this convention, John C. Fremont, a plausible political pretender, was nominated for the Presidency. As a candidate for Presidential elector, Lincoln again took the field. He made a thorough and energetic canvass, and his greatly improved powers of oratory now manifested themselves. Probably no man in the country, says Lamon, discussed the main questions at issue in a manner more original and persuasive. Buchanan, the Democratic candidate, was elected by a small majority. The Republican vote was largely increased by many offensive and inhuman enforcements of the fugitive slave law,[1] for it seemed at this time as if the South had gone mad, and was resolved to do all in its power to irritate the North into war.

On March 4th, 1857, Buchanan, the last Slave-President, was inaugurated, and, a few days after, Judge Taney, of the Supreme Court, rendered the famous "Dred Scott" decision relative to a fugitive negro slave of that name, to the effect that a man of African slave descent could not be a citizen of the United States—that the prohibition of slavery was

---

[1] Arnold, p. 95.

unconstitutional, and that it existed by the Constitution in all the territories. Judge Taney, in fact, declared that the negro had no rights which the white man was bound to respect. "Against the Constitution—against the memory of the nation—against a previous decision—against a series of enactments—he decided that the slave is property, and that the Constitution upholds it against every other property."[1] This decision was regarded as an outrage even by many old Democrats. In the same year the slavery-party in Kansas passed, by fraud and violence, the celebrated Lecompton Constitution, upholding slavery. By this time, Judge Douglas, the author of all this mischief, wishing to be re-elected to the Senate, and finding that there was no chance for him as a pro-slavery candidate, was suddenly seized with indignation at the Lecompton affair, which he pronounced an outrage. The result was the division of the Democratic party. He then made a powerful speech at Springfield, defending his course with great shrewdness, but it was, as usual, blown to the winds by a reply from Lincoln. Douglas suddenly became a zealous "Free Soiler," after the manner admirably burlesqued by "Petroleum Nasby,"[2] when that worthy found it was necessary

---

[1] George Bancroft, "Oration on Lincoln," pp. 13, 14.

[2] David R. Locke, who, under the name of Petroleum V. Nasby, wrote political satires much admired by Mr. Lincoln.

to become an anti-slavery man to keep his post-office. At this time Douglas made his famous assertion that he did not care whether slavery was voted up or down; and in the following year, April 30th, 1858, Congress passed the English Bill, by which the people of Kansas were offered heavy bribes in land if they would accept the Lecompton Constitution, but which the people rejected by an immense majority.

On the 16th June, 1858, a Republican State Convention at Springfield nominated Lincoln for the Senate, and on the 17th he delivered a bold speech, soon to be known far and wide as the celebrated "House divided against itself" speech. It began with these words—

"If we could first know where we are, and whither we are tending, we could then better judge what to do, and how to do it. We are now far on into the fifth year since a policy was initiated with the avowed object and confident promise of putting an end to slavery agitation. Under the operation of that policy, that agitation had not only not ceased, but has constantly augmented. In my opinion, it will not cease until a crisis shall have been reached and passed. 'A house divided against itself cannot stand.' I believe this Government cannot endure permanently, half slave and half free. I do not expect the Union to be dissolved—I do not expect the house to fall—but I do expect it will cease to be divided. It will become all one thing or all the other. Either the opponents of slavery will arrest the further spread of it, and place it where the public mind shall rest in the belief that it is in the course of ultimate extinction, or its advocates will push it forward till it shall become alike lawful in all the States—old as well as new, North as well as South.

"Have we no tendency to the latter condition? Let any one who doubts carefully contemplate that now almost complete legal combination—piece of machinery, so to speak—compounded of the Nebraska doctrine and the Dred Scott decision. Let him consider not only what work the machinery is adapted to do, and how well adapted, but also let him study the history of its construction, and trace, if he can, or rather fail, if he can, to trace the evidences of design and concert of action among its chief master-workers from the beginning."

These were awful words to the world, and with awe were they received. Lincoln was the first man among the "moderates" who had dared to speak so plainly. His friends were angry, but in due time this tremendous speech had the right effect, for it announced the truth. Meanwhile, Lincoln and Douglas were again paired together as rivals, and at one place the latter put to his adversary a series of questions, which were promptly answered. In return, Lincoln gave Douglas four others, by one of which he was asked if the people of a United States territory could in any lawful way, against the wish of any citizen of the United States, exclude slavery from its limits? To which Douglas replied that the people of a territory *had* the lawful means to exclude slavery by legislative action. This reply brought Douglas into direct antagonism with the pro-slavery men. He hoped, by establishing a "platform" of his own, to head so many Democrats that the Republicans would welcome his accession, and make him President. But Lincoln, by these questions, and by his unyielding attacks, weakened him to his ruin. It is true that Judge Douglas gained his seat in the Senate, but it was by an old and unjust law in the Legislature, as Lincoln really had four thousand majority.

The speeches which Lincoln delivered during this campaign, and which were afterwards published with those of Douglas, were so refined and masterly that many believed they had been revised for him by able friends. But from this time all his oratory indicated an advance in all respects. He was now bent on great things.

CHAPTER V.

Causes of Lincoln's Nomination to the Presidency—His Lectures in New York, &c.—The first Nomination and the Fence Rails—The Nomination at Chicago — Elected President — Office-seekers and Appointments—Lincoln's Impartiality—The South determined to Secede—Fears for Lincoln's Life.

IT is an almost invariable law of stern equity in the United States, as it must be in all true republics, that the citizen who has distinguished himself by great services must not expect really great rewards. The celebrity which he has gained seems, in a commonwealth, where all are ambitious of distinction, to be sufficient recompense. It is true that at times some overwhelming favourite, generally a military hero, is made an exception; but there are few very ambitious civilians who do not realise that a prophet is without great honour in his own country. Other instances may occur where aspiring men have carefully concealed their hopes, and of such was Abraham Lincoln. Perhaps his case is best stated by Lamon, who declares that he had all the requisites of an available candidate for the Presidency, chiefly because he had not been sufficiently prominent in national politics to excite the jealousies of powerful rivals. In order to defeat one another, these rivals will put forward some comparatively unknown man, and thus Lincoln was greatly indebted to the jealousy with which Horace Greeley, a New York politician, regarded his rival, W. H. Seward. Lincoln's abilities were very great, "but he knew that becoming modesty in a great man was about as needful as anything else." Therefore, when his friend Pickett suggested that he might aspire to the Chief Magistracy, he replied, "I do not think I am fit for the Presidency."

But he had friends who thought differently, and in the winter of 1859, Jackson Grimshaw, Mr. Hatch, the Secretary of State, and Messrs. Bushnell, Judd, and Peck, held a meeting, and, after a little persuasion, induced Lincoln to allow them to put him forward as a candidate for the great office. In October, 1859, Lincoln received an invitation from a committee of citizens to give a lecture in New York.[1] He was much pleased with this intimation that he was well known in "the East," and wrote out with great care a political address, which, when delivered, was warmly praised by the newspapers, one of which, the "Tribune," edited by Horace Greeley, declared that no man ever before made such an impression on his first appeal to a New York audience. The subject of the discourse was a most logical, vigorous, and masterly comment upon an assertion which Judge Douglas had made, to the effect that the framers

---

[1] See Appendix.

of the Constitution had understood and approved of slavery. No better vindication of the rights of the Republican party to be considered as expressing and carrying out in all respects the opinions of Washington and of the framers of the Constitution, was ever set forth. From New York he went to New England, lecturing in many cities, and everywhere verifying what was said of him in the "Manchester Mirror," that he spoke with great fairness, candour, and with wonderful interest. "He did not abuse the South, the Administration, or the Democrats. He is far from prepossessing in personal appearance, and his voice is disagreeable, yet he wins your attention and good-will from the start. His sense of the ludicrous is very keen, and an exhibition of that is the clincher of all his arguments—not the ludicrous acts of persons, but ludicrous ideas. Hence he is never offensive, and steals away willingly into his train of belief persons who were opposed to him. For the first half-hour his opponents would agree with every word he uttered, and from that point he began to lead them off, little by little, until it seemed as if he had got them all into his fold."

Lincoln was now approaching with great rapidity the summit of his wishes. On May 9th and 10th the Republican State Convention met at Springfield for the purpose of nominating a candidate for the Presidency, and it is said that Lincoln did not appear to have had any idea that any business relative to himself was to be transacted. For it is unquestionable that, while very ambitious, he was at the same time remarkably modest. When he went to lecture in New York, and the press reporters asked him for "slips," or copies of his speech, he was astonished, not feeling sure whether the newspapers would care to publish it. At this Convention, he was "sitting on his heels" in a back part of the room, and the Governor of Illinois, as soon as the meeting was organised, rose and said—"I am informed that a distinguished citizen of Illinois, and one whom Illinois will ever delight to honour, is present, and I wish to move that this body invite him to a seat on the stand." And, pausing, he exclaimed, "Abraham Lincoln." There was tremendous applause, and the mob seizing Lincoln, raised him in their arms, and bore him, sturdily resisting, to the platform. A gentleman who was present said—"I then thought him one of the most diffident and worst-plagued men I ever saw." The next proceeding was most amusing and characteristic, it being the entrance of "Old John Hanks," with two fence-rails bearing the inscription—*Two Rails from a lot made by Abraham Lincoln and John Hanks in the Sangamon bottom in the year 1830.* The end was that Lincoln was the declared candidate of his state for the Presidency.

But there were other candidates from other states, and at the great Convention in Chicago, on May 16th, there was as fierce intriguing and as much shrewdness shown as ever attended the election of a Pope. After publishing the "platform," or declaration of the principles of the Republican party—which was in the main a stern denunciation of all further extension of slavery—with a declaration in favour of protection, the rights of foreign citizens, and a Pacific railroad, the Convention proceeded to the main business. It was soon apparent that the real strife lay between W. H. Seward, of New York, and Abraham Lincoln. It would avail little to expose all the influences of trickery and enmity resorted to by the friends of either candidate on this occasion—suffice it to say that, eventually, Lincoln received the nomination, which was the prelude to the most eventful election ever witnessed in America. What followed has been well described by Lamon.

"All that day, and all the day previous, Mr. Lincoln was at Springfield, trying to behave as usual, but watching, with nervous anxiety, the proceedings of the Convention as they were reported by telegraph. On both days he played a great deal at fives in a ball-alley. It is probable that he took this physical mode of working off or keeping down the excitement that threatened to possess him. About nine o'clock in the morning, Mr. Lincoln came to the office of Lincoln and Herndon. Mr. Baker entered, with a telegram which said the names of the candidates had been announced, and that Mr. Lincoln's had been received with more applause than any other. When the news of the first ballot came over the wire, it was apparent to all present that Mr. Lincoln thought it very favourable. He believed if Mr. Seward failed to get the nomination, or to come very near it, on the first ballot, he would fail altogether. Presently, news of the second ballot arrived, and then Mr. Lincoln showed by his manner that he considered the contest no longer doubtful. 'I've got him,' said he. When the decisive despatch at length arrived, there was great commotion. Mr. Lincoln seemed to be calm, but a close observer could detect in his countenance the indications of deep emotion. In the meantime, cheers for Lincoln swelled up from the streets, and began to be heard through the town. Some one remarked, 'Mr. Lincoln, I suppose now we will soon have a book containing your life.' 'There is not much,' he replied, 'in my past life about which to write a book, as it seems to me.' Having received the hearty congratulations of the company in the office, he descended to the street, where he was immediately surrounded by Irish and American citizens; and, so long as he was willing to receive it, there was great hand-shaking and felicitating. 'Gentlemen,' said the great man, with a happy twinkle in his eye, 'you had better come up and shake my hand while you can; honours elevate some men, you know.' But he soon bethought him of a person who was of more importance to him than all this crowd. Looking towards his house, he said—'Well, gentlemen, there is a little short woman at our house who is probably more interested in this despatch than I am; and, if you will excuse me, I will take it up and let her see it.'"

The division caused by Douglas in the Democratic party to further his own personal ambition, utterly destroyed its power for a long time. The result was a division—one convention nominating Judge Douglas for the Presidency, with Mr. Johnson, of Georgia, as Vice-President; and the other, John C. Breckinridge, of Kentucky, with Joseph Lane, of Oregon, for the second office. Still another party, the Constitutional Union party, nominated John Bell, of Tennessee, and Edward Everett, of Massachusetts, for President and Vice-President. Thus there were four rival armies in the political field, soon to be merged into two in real strife. On Nov. 6th, 1860, Abraham Lincoln was elected President of the United States, receiving 1,857,610 votes; Douglas had 1,291,574; Breckinridge, 850,082; Bell, 646,124. Of all the votes really cast, there was a majority of 930,170 against Lincoln—a fact which was afterwards continually urged by the Southern party, which called him the Minority President. But when the electors who are chosen to elect the President met, they gave Lincoln 180 votes; Breckinridge, 72; Bell, 30; while Douglas, who might, beyond question, have been the successful candidate had he been less crafty, received only 12. The strife between him and Lincoln had been like that between the giant and the hero in the Norse mythology, wherein the two gave to each other riddles, on the successful answers to which their lives depended. Judge Douglas strove to entrap Lincoln with a long series of questions which were easily eluded, but one was demanded of the questioner himself, and the answer he gave to it proved his destruction.

The immediate result of Lincoln's election was such a rush of hungry politicians seeking office as had never before been witnessed. As every appointment in the United States, from the smallest post-office to a Secretaryship, is in the direct gift of the President, the newly-elected found himself attacked by thousands of place-hunters, ready to prove that they were the most deserving men in the world for reward; and if they did not, as "Artemus Ward" declares, come down the chimneys of the White House to interview him, they at least besieged him with such pertinacity, and made him so thoroughly wretched, that he is said to have at last replied to one man who insisted that it was really to his

exertions that the President owed his election—
"If that be so, I wonder you are not ashamed to
look me in the face for getting me into such an
abominable situation."

From his own good nature, and from a sincere
desire to really deserve his popular name of Honest
Old Abe, Lincoln determined to appoint the best
men to office, irrespective of party. Hoping against
hope to preserve the Union, he would have given
place in his Cabinet to Southern Democrats as well
as to Northern Republicans. But as soon as it was
understood that he was elected, and that the country
would have a President opposed to the extension
of slavery, the South began to prepare to leave the
Union, and for war. It was in vain that Lincoln
and the great majority of his party made it clear
as possible that, rather than see the country destroyed
by war and by disunion, they would leave slavery as
it was. This did not suit the views of the "rule-or-
ruin" party of the South; and as secession from the
Federal Union became a fixed fact, their entire press
and all their politicians declared that their object was
not merely to build up a Southern Confederacy, but
to legislate so as to destroy the industry of the North,
and break the old Union into a thousand conflicting
independent governments. Therefore, Lincoln, in
intending to offer seats in the Cabinet to Alexander
H. Stephens, James Guthrie, of Kentucky, and John

A. Gilmer, of North Carolina, made—if sincere—a great mistake, though one in every way creditable to his heart and his courtesy. The truth was, that the South had for four years unanimously determined to secede, and was actually seceding; while the North, which had gone beyond the extreme limits of endurance and of justice itself to conciliate the South, could not believe that fellow-countrymen and brothers seriously intended war. For it was predetermined and announced by the Southern press that, unless the Federal Government would make concessions beyond all reason, and put itself in the position of a disgraced and conquered state, there must be war.

As the terrible darkness began to gather, and the storm-signals to appear, Lincoln sought for temporary relief in visiting his stepmother and other old friends and relatives in Coles County. The meeting with her whom he had always regarded as his mother was very touching; it was the more affecting because she, to whom he was the dearest on earth, was under an impression, which time rendered prophetic, that he would, as President, be assassinated. This anticipation spread among his friends, who vied with one another in gloomy suggestions of many forms of murder—while one very zealous prophet, who had fixed on poison as the means by which Lincoln would die, urged him to take as a cook from home "one among his own female friends."

CHAPTER VI.

A Suspected Conspiracy—Lincoln's Departure for Washington—His Speeches at Springfield and on the road to the National Capital—Breaking out of the Rebellion—Treachery of President Buchanan—Treason in the Cabinet—Jefferson Davis's Message—Threats of Massacre and Ruin to the North—Southern Sympathisers—Lincoln's Inaugural Address—The Cabinet—The Days of Doubt and of Darkness.

IT was unfortunate for Lincoln that he listened to the predictions of his alarmed friends. So generally did the idea prevail that an effort would be made to kill him on his way to Washington, that a few fellows of the lower class in Baltimore, headed by a barber named Ferrandina, thinking to gain a little notoriety—as they actually did get some money from Southern sympathisers—gave out that they intended to murder Mr. Lincoln on his journey to Washington. Immediately a number of detectives was set to work; and as everybody seemed to wish to find a plot, a plot was found, or imagined, and Lincoln was persuaded to pass privately and disguised on a special train from Harrisburg, Pennsylvania, to Washington, where he arrived February 23rd, 1861. Before leaving Springfield, he addressed his friends at the moment of parting, at the railway station, in a speech of impressive simplicity.

"FRIENDS,—No one who has never been placed in a like position can understand my feelings at this hour, nor the oppressive sadness I feel at this parting. For more than a quarter of a century I have lived among you, and during all that time I have received nothing but kindness at your hands. Here I have lived from youth until now I am an old man; here the most sacred ties of earth were assumed; here all my children were born, and here one of them lies buried. To you, dear friends, I owe all that I have, all that I am. All the strange, chequered past seems now to crowd upon my mind. To-day I leave you. I go to assume a task more difficult than that which devolved upon Washington. Unless the great God who assisted him shall be with me and aid me, I must fail; but if the same omniscient mind and almighty arm that directed and protected him shall guide and support me, I shall not fail—I shall succeed. Let us all pray that the God of our fathers may not forsake us now. To Him I commend you all. Permit me to ask that with equal sincerity and faith you will invoke His wisdom and guidance for me. With these few words I must leave you, for how long I know not. Friends, one and all, I must now bid you an affectionate farewell."

It may be observed that in this speech Lincoln, notwithstanding his conciliatory offers to the South, apprehended a terrible war, and that when speaking from the heart he showed himself a religious man. If he ever spoke in earnest it was on this occasion. One who had heard him a hundred times declared that he never saw him so profoundly affected, nor did he ever utter an address which seemed so full of simple and touching eloquence as this. It left his audience deeply affected; but the same people were more deeply moved at his return. "At eight o'clock," says Lamon, "the train rolled out of Springfield amid the cheers of the populace. Four years later, a funeral train, covered with the emblems of splendid mourning, rolled into the same city, bearing a corpse, whose obsequies were being celebrated in every part of the civilised world."

Lincoln made several speeches at different places along his route from Springfield to Philadelphia, and in all he freely discussed the difficulties of the political crisis, expressing himself to the effect that there was really no danger or no crisis, since he was resolved, with all the Union-loving men of the North, to grant the South all its rights. But these addresses were not all sugar and rose-water. At Philadelphia he said—

"Now, in my view of the present aspect of affairs, there need be no bloodshed or war. There is no necessity for it. I am not in favour of such a course; and I may say in advance, that there will be no blood shed, unless it be forced upon the Government, and then it will be compelled to act in self-defence."

Lincoln had declared that the duties which would devolve upon him would be greater than those which had devolved upon any American since Washington. During this journey, the wisdom, firmness, and ready tact of his speeches already indicated that he would perform these duties of statesmanship in a masterly manner. He was received courteously by immense multitudes; but at this time so very little was known of him beyond the fact that he was called Honest Old Abe the Rail-splitter, and that he had sprung from that most illiterate source, a poor Southern backwoods family, that even his political friends went to hear him with misgivings or with shame. There was a general impression that the Republican party had gained a victory by truckling to the mob, and by elevating one of its roughest types to leadership. And the gaunt, uncouth appearance of the President-elect fully confirmed this opinion. But when he spoke, it was as if a spell had been removed; the disguise of Odin fell away, and people knew the Great Man, called to struggle with and conquer the rebellious giants—a hero coming with the right strength at the right time.

It was at this time that the conspiracy, which had been preparing in earnest for thirty years, and which the North for as many years refused to suspect, had burst forth. South Carolina had declared that if Lincoln was elected she would secede, and on the 17th December, 1860, she did so, true to her word if not to her duty. In quick succession six States followed her, "there being little or no struggle, in those which lay upon the Gulf, against the wild tornado of excitement in favour of rebellion." "In the Border States," says Arnold—"in Maryland, Virginia, North Carolina, Tennessee, and Missouri—there was, however, a terrible contest." The Union ultimately triumphed in Maryland, Kentucky, and Missouri, while the rebels carried Tennessee with great difficulty. Virginia seceded on April 17th, 1861, and North Carolina on the 20th of May. Everything had for years been made ready for them. President Buchanan, who preceded Lincoln—a man of feeble mind, and entirely devoted to the South—had either suffered the rebels to do all in their power to facilitate secession, or had directly aided them. The Secretary of War, John B. Floyd, who became a noted rebel, had for months been at work to paralyse the Northern army. He ordered 115,000 muskets to be made in Northern arsenals at the expense of the Federal Government, and sent them all to the South, with vast numbers of cannon, mortars, ammunition, and munitions of war. The army, reduced to 16,000 men, was sent to remote parts of the country, and as the great majority of its officers were Southern men, they of course resigned their commissions, and went over to the Southern Confederacy. Howell Cobb of Georgia, afterwards a rebel general, was Secretary of the Treasury, and, as his contribution to the Southern cause, did his utmost, and with great success, to cause ruin in his department, to injure the national credit, and empty the treasury. In fact, the whole Cabinet, with the supple

President for a willing tool, were busy for months in doing all in their power to utterly break up the Government, to support which they had pledged their faith in God and their honour as gentlemen. Linked with them in disgrace were all those who, after uniting in holding an election for President, refused to abide by its results. On the 20th Nov., 1860, the Attorney-General of the United States, Jer. S. Black, gave, as his aid to treason, the official opinion that "Congress had no right to carry on war against any State, either to prevent a threatened violation of the Constitution, or to enforce an acknowledgment that the Government of the United States was supreme;" and to use the words of Raymond, "it soon became evident that the President adopted this theory as the basis and guide of his executive action."

On the night of January 5th, 1861, the leading conspirators, Jefferson Davis, with Senators Toombs, Iverson, Slidell, Benjamin, Wigfall, and others, held a meeting, at which it was resolved that the South should secede, but that all the seceding senators and representatives should retain their seats as long as possible, in order to inflict injury to the last on the Government which they had officially pledged themselves to protect. At the suggestion probably of Mr. Benjamin, all who retired were careful to draw not only their pay, but also to spoil the Egyptians by taking all the stationery, documents, and "mileage," or allowance for travelling expenses, on which they could lay their hands. Only two of all the Slave State representatives remained true—Mr. Bouligny from New Orleans, and Andrew J. Hamilton from Texas. When President Lincoln came to Washington, it was indeed to enter a house divided against itself, tottering to its fall, its inner chambers a mass of ruin.

The seven States which had seceded sent delegates, which met at Montgomery, Alabama, February 4th, 1861, and organised a government and constitution similar to that of the United States, under which Jefferson Davis was President, and Alexander H. Stephens Vice-President. No one had threatened the new Southern Government, and at this stage the North would have suffered it to withdraw in peace from the Union, so great was the dread of a civil war. But the South did not want peace. Every Southern newspaper, every rebel orator, was now furiously demanding of the North the most humiliating concessions, and threatening bloodshed as the alternative. While President Lincoln, in his Inaugural Address, spoke with the most Christian forbearance of the South, Jefferson Davis, in his, assumed all the horrors of civil war as a foregone conclusion. He said, that if they were permitted to secede quietly, all would be well. If forced to fight, they could and would maintain their position by the sword, and would avail themselves to the utmost of the liberties of war. He expected that the North would be the theatre of war, but no Northern city ever felt the rebel sword, while there was not one in the South which did not suffer terribly from the effects of war. Never in history was the awful curse *Væ victis* so freely invoked by those who were destined to be conquered.

It was characteristic of Lincoln to illustrate his views on all subjects by anecdotes, which were so aptly put as to present in a few words the full force of his argument. Immediately after his election, when the world was vexed with the rumours of war, he was asked what he intended to do when he got to Washington? "That," he replied, "puts me in mind of a little story. There was once a clergyman, who expected during the course of his next day's riding to cross the Fox River, at a time when the stream would be swollen by a spring freshet, making the passage extremely dangerous. On being asked by anxious friends if he was not afraid, and what he intended to do, the clergyman calmly replied, 'I have travelled this country a great deal, and I can assure you that I have no intention of trying to cross Fox River *until I get to it.*'" The dangers of the political river which Mr. Lincoln was to cross were very great. It is usual in England to regard the struggle of the North with the South during the Rebellion as that of a great power with a lesser one, and sympathy was in consequence given to the so-called weaker side. But the strictest truth shows that the Union party, what with the Copperheads, or sympathisers with the South, at home, and with open foes in the field, was never at any time much more than equal to either branch of the enemy, and that, far from being the strongest in numbers, it was as one to two. Those in its ranks who secretly aided the enemy were numerous and powerful. The Union armies were sometimes led by generals whose hearts were with the foe; and for months after the war broke out, the entire telegraph service of the Union was, owing to the treachery of officials, entirely at the service of the Confederates.

It must be fairly admitted, and distinctly borne in mind, that the South had at least good apparent reason for believing that the North would yield to any demands, and was so corrupt that it would crumble at a touch into numberless petty, warring States, while the Confederacy, firm and united, would eventually master them all, and rule the Continent. For years, leaders like President Buchanan had been their most submissive tools; and the number of men in the North who were willing to grant them everything very nearly equalled that of the Republican party. From the beginning they were assured by the press and leaders of the Democrats, or Copperheads, that they would soon conquer, and receive material aid from Northern sympathisers. And there were in all the Northern cities many of these, who were eagerly awaiting a breaking-up of the Union, in order that they might profit by its ruin. Thus, immediately after the secession of South Carolina, Fernando Wood, Mayor of New York, issued a proclamation, in which he recommended that it should secede, and become a "free city." All over the country, Democrats like Wood were looking forward to revolutions in which something might be picked up, and not a few really spoke of the revival of titles of nobility. All of these prospective governors of lordly Baratarias avowed sympathy with the South. It was chiefly by reliance on these Northern sympathisers that the Confederacy was led to its ruin. President Lincoln found himself in command of a beleagured fortress which had been systematically stripped and injured by his predecessor, a powerful foe storming without, and nearly half his men doing their utmost to aid the enemy from within.

On the 4th March, 1861, Lincoln took the oath to fulfil his duties as President, and delivered his inaugural address. In this he began by asserting that he had no intention of interfering with slavery as it existed, or of interfering in any way with the rights of the South, and urged that, by law, fugitive slaves must be restored to their owners. In reference to the efforts being made to break up the Union, he maintained that, by universal law and by the Constitution, the union of the States must be perpetual.

"It is safe to assert," he declared, "that no government proper ever had a provision in its organic law for its own termination." With great wisdom, and in the most temperate language, he pointed out the impossibility of any *government*, in the true sense of the word, being liable to dissolution because a party wished it. One party to a contract may violate or break it, but it requires all to lawfully rescind it.

"I therefore consider that, in view of the Constitution and the laws, the Union is unbroken; and to the extent of my ability, I shall take care, as the Constitution itself expressly enjoins upon me, that the laws of the Union be faithfully executed in all the States. Doing this I deem to be only a simple duty on my part; and I shall perform it as far as practicable, unless my rightful masters, the American people, shall withhold the requisite means, or in some authoritative manner direct the contrary."

He asserted that the power confided to him would be used to hold and possess all Government property and collect duties; but went so far in conciliation as to declare, that wherever hostility to the United States should be so great and universal as to prevent competent resident citizens from holding the Federal offices, there would be no attempt to force obnoxious strangers among the people for that object. Where the enforcement of such matters, though legally right, might be irritating and nearly impracticable, he would deem it better to forego for a time the uses of such offices. He pointed out that the principle of secession was simply that of anarchy; that to admit the claim of a minority would be to destroy any government; while he indicated with great intelligence the precise limits of the functions of the Supreme Court. And he briefly explained the impossibility of a divided Union existing, save in a jarring and ruinous manner. "Physically speaking," he said, "we cannot separate. We cannot remove our respective sections from each other, nor build an impassable wall between them. A husband and wife may be divorced, and go out of the presence and beyond the reach of each other, but the different parts of our country cannot do this. They cannot but remain face to face; and intercourse either amicable or hostile must continue between them. Why should there not be," he added, "a patient confidence in the ultimate justice of the people? Is there any better or equal hope in the world? In our present differences, is either party without faith of being in the right? If the Mighty Ruler of Nations, with His eternal truth and justice, be on your side of the North, or on yours of the South, that truth and that justice will surely prevail by the judgment of this great tribunal of the American people."

It has been well said that this address was the wisest utterance of the time. Yet it was, with all its gentle and conciliatory feelings, at once misrepresented through the South as a malignant and tyrannical threat of war; for to such a pitch of irritability and arrogance had the entire Southern party been raised, that any words from a Northern ruler, not expressive of the utmost devotion to their interests, seemed literally like insult. It was not enough to promise them to be bound by law, when they held that the only law should be their own will.

To those who lived through the dark and dreadful days which preceded the outburst of the war, every memory is like that of one who has passed through the valley of the shadow of death. It was known that the enemy was coming from abroad; yet there were few who could really regard him as an enemy, for it was as when a brother advances to slay a brother, and the victim, not believing in the threat, rises to throw himself into the murderer's arms. And vigorous defence was further paralysed by the feeling that traitors were everywhere at work—in the army, in the Cabinet, in the family circle.

President Lincoln proceeded at once to form his Cabinet. It consisted of William H. Seward—who had been his most formidable competitor at the Chicago Convention—who became Secretary of State; Simon Cameron—whose appointment proved as discreditable to Mr. Lincoln as to the country—as Secretary of War; Salmon P. Chase, Secretary of the Treasury; Gideon Welles, Secretary of the Navy; Caleb B.

Smith, Secretary of the Interior; Montgomery Blair, Postmaster-General; and Edward Bates, Attorney-General. It was well for the President that these were all, except Cameron, wise and honest men, for the situation of the country was one of doubt, danger, and disorganisation. In Congress, in every drawing-room, there were people who boldly asserted and believed in the words of a rebel, expressed to B. F. Butler—that "the North could not fight; that the South had too many allies there." "You have friends," said Butler, "in the North who will stand by you as long as you fight your battles in the Union; but the moment you fire on the flag, the Northern people will be a unit against you. And you may be assured, if war comes, slavery *ends*." Orators and editors in the North proclaimed, in the boldest manner, that the Union must go to fragments and ruin, and that the only hope of safety lay in suffering the South to take the lead, and in humbly following her. The number of these despairing people—or Croakers, as they were called—was very great; they believed that Republicanism had proved itself a failure, and that on slavery alone could a firm government be based. Open treason was unpunished; it was boldly said that Southern armies would soon be on Northern soil; the New Administration seemed to be without a basis; in those days, no men except rebels seemed to know what to do.

CHAPTER VII.

Mr. Seward refuses to meet the Rebel Commissioners—Lincoln's Forbearance—Fort Sumter—Call for 75,000 Troops—Troubles in Maryland—Administrative Prudence—Judge Douglas—Increase of the Army—Winthrop and Ellsworth—Bull Run—General M'Clellan.

IT was on the 12th of March, 1861, that the rebel or Confederate States sent Commissioners to the United States to adjust matters in reference to secession. Mr. Seward refused to receive them, on the ground that they *had not withdrawn* from the Union, and were unable to do so unless it were by the authority of a National Convention acting according to the Constitution of the United States. On the 9th of April the Commissioners left, declaring in a letter that "they accepted the gage of battle." As yet there was no decided policy in the North, and prominent Democrats like Douglas were not in favour of compelling the seceding States to remain. Mr. Everett was preaching love, forgiveness, and union, while the Confederate Government was seizing on "all the arsenals, forts, custom-houses, post-offices, ships, ordnance, and material of war belonging to the United States, within the seceding States." In fact, the South knew exactly what it meant to do, and was doing it vigorously, while the North was entirely undecided. In the spring of 1861, Congress had adjourned without making any preparation for the tremendous and imminent crisis.

But the entire South had not as yet seceded. The Border States were not in favour of war. In the words of Arnold, "to arouse sectional feeling and prejudice, and secure co-operation and unanimity, it was deemed necessary to precipitate measures and bring on a conflict of arms." It was generally felt that the first blood shed would bring all the Slave States into union. The anti-war party was so powerful in the North, that it now appears almost certain that, if President Lincoln had proceeded at once to put down the rebellion with a strong hand, there would have been a counter-rebellion in the North. For not doing this he was bitterly blamed, but time has justified him. By his forbearance, Maryland, Kentucky, and Missouri were undoubtedly kept in the Federal Union. His wisdom was also shown in two other respects, as soon as it was possible to do so. There had existed for years in New York an immense slave-trading business, headed by a Spaniard named Juarez. Vessels were bought almost openly, and Government officials were bribed to let these pirates loose. This infamous traffic was very soon brought to an end, so far as the United States were concerned. Another task, which was rapidly and well performed, was the "sifting out" of rebels, or rebel sympathisers, from Government offices, where they abounded and acted as spies. Even General Scott, an old man full of honour, who was at the head of the army, though true to the Union, was Southern by sympathy and opposed to coercion, and most of the officers of the army were like him in this respect.

The refusal of Mr. Seward to treat with the rebel government was promptly made the occasion for the act of violence which was to unite the Confederacy. There was, near Charleston, South Carolina, a fort called Sumter, held for the United States by Major Robert Anderson, a brave and loyal man. On the 11th of April, 1861, he was summoned to surrender the fort to the Confederate Government, which he refused to do. As he was, however, without provisions, it was eventually agreed, on the 12th April, that he should leave the fort by noon on the 15th. But the rebels, in their impatience, could not wait, and they informed him that, unless he surrendered within one hour, the fort would be bombarded. This was done, and, after a bombardment of thirty-three hours, bravely borne, the Major and his band of seventy men were obliged to surrender.

It is true that this first firing on the American flag acted like the tap of the drum, calling all the South to arms in a frenzy, and sweeping away all the remnants of attachment to the old Union lingering in it. The utmost hopes of the rebel leaders were for the time fully realised. But the North was, to their amazement, not paralysed or struck down, nor did the Democratic sympathisers with the South arise and crush "Lincoln and his minions." On the contrary, the news of the fall of Sumter was "a live coal on the heart of the American people;" and such a tempest of rage swept in a day over millions, as had never before been witnessed in America. Those who can recall the day on which the news of the insult to the flag was received, and how it was received, have the memory of the greatest conceivable outburst of patriotic passion. For a time, all party feelings were forgotten; there was no more thought of forgiveness, or suffering secession; the whole people rose up and cried out for war.

Hitherto, the press had railed at Lincoln for wanting a policy; and yet if he had made one step towards suppressing the rebels, "a thousand Northern newspapers would have pounced upon him as one provoking war." Now, however, his policy was formed, shaped, and made glowing hot by one terrible blow. On April 15th, 1861, he issued a proclamation, announcing that, as the laws of the United States were being opposed, and the execution thereof obstructed in South Carolina, Georgia, Alabama, Florida, Mississippi, Louisiana, and Texas, by combinations too powerful to be suppressed by the ordinary course of judicial proceedings; he, the President of the United States, called forth the militia of the several States of the Union, to the aggregate number of 75,000, in order to suppress said combinations, and to cause the laws to be duly executed. In strong contrast to the threats of general slaughter, and conflagration of Northern cities, so freely thrown out by Jefferson Davis, President Lincoln declared that, while the duty of these troops would be to repossess the forts and property taken from the Union, "in every event the utmost care will be observed, consistently with the objects aforesaid, to avoid any devastation, any destruction of or interference with property, or any disturbance of peaceful citizens, in any part of the country." He also summoned an extraordinary session of Congress to assemble on the 4th of July, 1861.

This proclamation awoke intense enthusiasm, "and from private persons, as well as by the Legislature, men, arms, and money were offered in unstinted profusion in support of the Government. Massachusetts was first in the field; and on the first day after the issue of the proclamation, the 6th Regiment started from Boston for the national capital. Two more regiments departed within forty-eight hours. The 6th Regiment, on its way to Washington, on the 19th April, was attacked by a mob in Baltimore, carrying a secession flag, and several of its members were killed." This inflamed to a higher point the entire North; and Governor Hicks, of Maryland, and Mayor Brown, of Baltimore, urged it on President Lincoln that, "for prudential reasons," no more troops should be sent through Baltimore. This Governor Hicks had, during the previous November, written a letter, in which he regretted that his state could not supply the rebel states with arms more rapidly, and expressed the hope that those who were to bear them would be "good men to kill Lincoln and his men." But by adroitly shifting to the wind, he "became conspicuously loyal before spring, and lived to reap splendid rewards and high honours under the auspices of the Federal Government, as the most patriotic and devoted Union-man in Maryland." Yet as one renegade is said to be more zealous than ten Turks, it cannot be denied that, after Governor Hicks became a Union-man, he worked bravely, and his efficiency in preserving Maryland from seceding was only inferior to that of the able Henry Winter Davis. This Governor Hicks had suggested to President Lincoln that the controversy between North and South might be referred to Lord Lyons, the British Minister, for arbitration. To these requests the President replied, through Mr. Seward, that as General Scott deemed it advisable, and as the chief object in bringing troops was the defence of Washington, he made no point of bringing them through Baltimore. But he concluded with these words—

"The President cannot but remember that there has been a time in the history of our country when a General of the American Union, with forces destined for the defence of its capital, was not unwelcome anywhere in the State of Maryland.

"If eighty years could have obliterated all the other noble sentiments of that age in Maryland, the President would be hopeful, nevertheless, that there is one that would for ever remain there and everywhere. That sentiment is, that no domestic contention whatever that may arise among the parties of this republic ought in any case to be referred to any foreign arbitrament, least of all to the arbitrament of a European monarchy."

It is certain that by this humane and wise policy, which many attributed to cowardice, President Lincoln not only prevented much bloodshed and devastation, but also preserved the State of Maryland. In such a crisis harshly aggressive measures in Maryland would have irritated millions on the border, and perhaps have promptly brought the war further north. As it was, peace and order were soon restored in Baltimore, when the regular use of the highway through that city was resumed.

On the 19th April, 1861, the President issued another proclamation, declaring the blockade of the ports of the seceding states. This was virtually an answer to one from Jefferson Davis, offering letters of marque to all persons who might desire to aid the rebel government, and enrich themselves, by depredations upon the rich and extended commerce of the United States. It may be remarked that the first official words of Jefferson Davis were singularly ferocious, threatening fire, brigandage, and piracy, disguised as privateering, in all their terrors; while his last act as President was to run away, disguised as an old woman, in his wife's waterproof cloak, and carrying a bucket of water—thus typifying in his own person the history of the rebellion from its fierce beginning to its ignominious end.

It may be doubted if there was in those wild days in all North America one man who to such wise forbearance added such firmness and moral courage as President Lincoln manifested. By it he preserved Maryland, Kentucky, Tennessee, and Missouri, and, if moderation could have availed, he might have kept Virginia. Strange as it seems, while the seceding states were threatening officially, and hastening to carry out, all the outrages of war, the Legislature of Virginia resolved that President Lincoln's mild message announced a policy of tyranny and "coercion;" and, in spite of the gentlest letter of explanation ever written by any ruler who was not a coward, the state marched out of the Union with drums beating and flags flying. "Thenceforth," says Holland, "Virginia went straight towards desolation. Its 'sacred soil' was from that hour devoted to trenches, fortifications, battle-fields, military roads, camps, and graves." She firmly believed that all the fighting would be done on Northern soil; but in another year, over a large part of her territory, which had been covered with fertile farms and pleasant villages, there were roads five miles wide.

At this time, there occurred an interesting private incident in Lincoln's life. His old adversary, Judge Douglas, whom he warmly respected as a brave adversary, had passed his life in pandering to slavery, and, as regards the war, had been the political Mephistopheles who had made all the mischief. But when Sumter was fired on, all that was good and manly in his nature was aroused, and he gave all his support to his old enemy. "During the brief remainder of his life, his devotion to the cause of his country was unwearied. He was done with his dreams of power," but he could yet do good. He was of service in inducing great numbers of Democrats, who still remained pro-slavery men in principle, to fight for the Union.

Four years to an hour after the memorable reconciliation between Judge Douglas and President Lincoln, the latter was ●●●ed by the rebel Booth. "Both died," says Holland, "with a common purpose —one in the threatening morning of the rebellion, the other when its sun had just set in blood; and both sleep in the dust of that magnificent state, almost every rod of which, within a quarter of a century, had echoed to their contending voices, as they expounded their principles to the people."

Judge Douglas had warned the President, in the hour of their reconciliation, that, instead of calling on the country for 75,000 men, he should have asked for 200,000. "You do not know the dishonest purposes of those men as I do," he had impressively remarked. In a few days, it was evident that the rebellion was assuming colossal proportions, and therefore President Lincoln, on May 3rd, issued another call for 42,000 three-year volunteers, and ordered the addition of 22,114 officers and men to the regular army, and 18,000 seamen to the navy. This demand was promptly responded to, for the draft had as yet no terrors. On the 18th of April, a plot had been discovered by which the secessionists in Washington, aided by Virginia, hoped to fire the city, seize the President and Cabinet, and all the machinery of government. By prompt action, this plan was crushed. A part of it was to burn the railway bridges, and make the roads impassable, and this was successfully executed. Yet, in the face of this audacious attack, the Democratic press of the North and the rebel organs of the South continued to storm at the President for irritating the secessionists, declaring that "coercion" or resistance of the Federal Government to single states was illegal. But at this time several events occurred which caused great anger among loyal men: one was the loss of the great national armoury at Harper's Ferry, and also of Gosport Navy Yard, with 2000 cannon and several large ships. Owing to treachery, this navy yard, with about 10,000,000 dollars' worth of property, was lost. Another incident was the death of Colonel Ellsworth. This young man, who had been a law student under Mr. Lincoln, was the introducer of the Zouave drill. For many weeks, a rebel tavern-keeper in Alexandria, in sight of Washington, had insulted the Government by keeping a secession flag flying. On the 24th May, when General Mansfield advanced into Virginia, Ellsworth was sent with 13,000 troops to Alexandria. Here his first act was to pull down the rebel flag. On descending, Jackson shot him dead, and was himself promptly shot by private Brownell. Two days previous, the first considerable engagement of the war had occurred at Big Bethel, and here Major Winthrop, a young Massachusetts gentleman of great bravery and distinguished literary talent, was killed. The grief which the deaths of these well-known young men excited was very great. They were among the first victims, and their names remain to this day fresh in the minds of all who were in the

North during the war. The funeral of Ellsworth took place from the White House, Mr. Lincoln—who was affected with peculiar sorrow by his death—being chief mourner.

During this month the war was, to a degree, organised. As soon as Washington was made safe, Fortress Monroe, the "water-gateway" of Virginia, was reinforced. Cairo, Illinois, commanding the junction of the Mississippi and Ohio rivers, was occupied, and Virginia and North Carolina were efficiently blockaded. Pennsylvania, Delaware, Maryland, the District of Columbia, and a part of Virginia, were divided into three military departments, and on the 10th May another was formed, including the States of Ohio, Indiana, and Illinois, under charge of General Geo. B. M'Clellan. The object of this department was to maintain a defensive line on the Ohio River from Wheeling to Cairo.

In the month of July, 1861, the rebels, commanded by General Beauregard, threatened Washington, being placed along Bull Run Creek, their right resting on Manassas, and their left, under General Johnston, on Winchester. They numbered about 35,000. It was determined to attack this force, and drive it from the vicinity of Washington. Both sides intended this to be a great decisive battle, and it was generally believed in the North that it would end the war. Government had been supplied with men and money beyond its demands, and the people, encouraged by Mr. Seward's opinion that the war would last only sixty days, were as impatient now to end the rebellion by force as they had been previously to smother it by concessions. There were few who predicted as Charles A. Dana did to the writer, on the day that war was declared—that it would last "not less than three, nor more than six or seven years." On the 16th July, the Federal army, commanded by General M'Dowell, marched forth, and the attack, which was at first successful, was made on the 21st. But the reinforcements which Johnston received saved him, and a sudden panic sprung up among the Federal troops, which resulted in a headlong retreat, with 480 killed and 1000 wounded. The army was utterly beaten, and it was only the Confederates' ignorance of the extent of their own success which saved Washington. It was the darkest day ever witnessed in the North, when the telegraph announced the shameful defeat of the great army of the Union. Everyone had anticipated a brilliant victory; but yet the news discouraged no one. The writer that day observed closely the behaviour of hundreds of men as they came up to the bulletin-board of the New York *Times*, and can testify that, after a blank look of grief and amazement, they invariably spoke to this effect, "It's bad luck, but we must try it again." The effect, in the words of Raymond, was to rouse

War begins in Earnest.

still higher the courage and determination of the people. In twenty-four hours, the whole country was again fierce and fresh for war. Volunteers streamed by thousands into the army, and efforts were promptly made to establish Union forces at different places around the rebel coast. This was the beginning of the famous Anaconda, whose folds never relaxed until they strangled the rebellion. Between the 28th August and the 3rd of December, Fort Hatteras, Port Royal in South Carolina, and Ship Island, near New Orleans, were occupied. Preparations were made to seize on New Orleans; and, by a series of masterly movements, West Virginia, Kentucky, and Missouri, which had been in a painful state of conflict, were secured to the Union. Virginia proper had seceded with a flourish of States Rights. Her Western portion recognised the doctrine so far as to claim its right to leave the mother-state and return to the Union. This was not done without vigorous fighting by Generals Rosencranz and Morris, to whom the credit of both organising and acting is principally due, although General M'Clellan, by a clever and Napoleonic despatch, announcing victory, attracted to himself the chief glory. General M'Clellan had previously, in Kentucky, favoured the recognition of that state as neutral territory, as the rebels wished him to do—an attempt which Lincoln declared "would be disunion completed, if once entertained." On the

1st Nov., 1861, General Scott, who had hitherto commanded the armies of the Union, asked for and obtained his discharge, and was succeeded by General M'Clellan. "If," as Holland remarks, "he had done but little before to merit this confidence, if he did but little afterwards to justify it, he at least served at that time to give faith to the people." For three months he organised and supervised his troops with the talent which was peculiar to him—that of preparing great work for greater minds to finish. His photograph was in every album, and on every side were heard predictions that he would be the Napoleon, the Cæsar, the Autocrat of all the Americas. The Western Continent would be, after all, the greatest country in the world, and the greatest man in it was to be "Little Mac." He was not as yet known by his great botanical *nom de guerre* of the Virginian Creeper.

CHAPTER VIII.

Relations with Europe—Foreign Views of the War—The Slaves--Proclamation of Emancipation—Arrest of Rebel Commissioners—Black Troops.

WITH so much to call for his care in the field, President Lincoln was not less busy in the Cabinet. The relations of the Federal Government with Europe were of great importance. "The rebels," says Arnold, with truth, "had a positive, vigorous organisation, with agents all over Europe, many of them in the diplomatic service of the United States." They were well selected, and they were successful in creating the impression that the Confederacy was eminently "a gentleman's government"—that the Federal represented an agrarian mob led by demagogues—that Mr. Lincoln was a vulgar, ignorant boor—and that the war itself was simply an unconstitutional attempt to force certain states to remain under a tyrannical and repulsive rule. The great fact that the South had, in the most public manner, proclaimed that it seceded *because the North would not permit the further extension of slavery*, was utterly ignored; and the active interference of the North with slavery was ostentatiously urged as a grievance, though, by a strange inconsistency, it was deemed expedient by many foreign anti-slavery men to withdraw all sympathy for the Federal cause, on the ground that its leaders manifested no eagerness to set the slaves free until it became a matter of military expediency. Thus the humane wisdom and moderation, which inspired Lincoln and the true men of the Union to overcome the dreadful obstacles which existed in the opposition of the Northern democrats to Emancipation, was most sophistically and cruelly turned against them. To a more cynical class, the war was but the cleaning by fire of a filthy chimney which should have been burnt out long before, and its Iliad in a nutshell amounted to a squabble which concerned nobody save as a matter for amusement. And there were, finally, not a few—to judge from the frank avowal of a journal of the highest class—who looked forward with joy to the breaking up of the American Union, because "their sympathies were with men, not with monsters, and Russia and the United States are simply giants among nations." All this bore, in due time, its natural fruit. Whether people were to blame for this want of sympathy, considering the ingenuity with which Southern agents fulfilled their missions, is another matter. Time, which is, happily, every day modifying old feelings, cannot change truths.

And it cannot be denied that hostilities had hardly begun, and that only half the Slave States were in insurrection, when the English and French Governments, acting in concert, recognised the government at Montgomery as an established belligerent power. As to this recognition, Mr. Charles F. Adams, the United States Minister to England, was instructed by Mr. Seward to the effect that it, if carried out, must at once suspend all friendly relations between the United States and England. When, on June 15th, the English and French ministers applied to Mr. Seward for leave to communicate to him their instructions, directing them to recognise the rebels as belligerents, he declined to listen to them. The United States, accordingly, persisted until the end in regarding the rebellion as a domestic difficulty, and one with which foreign governments had no right to interfere. At the present day, it appears most remarkable that the two great sources of encouragement held out to the rebels—of help from Northern sympathisers, and the hope of full recognition by European powers—proved in the end to be allurements which led them on to ruin. Had it not been for the defeat at Bull Run, slavery would perhaps have still existed; and but for the hope of foreign aid, the South would never have been so utterly conquered and thoroughly exhausted as it was. It must, however, be admitted that the irritation of the Union-men of the North against England at this crisis was carried much too far, since they did not take fully into consideration the very large number of their sincere friends in Great Britain who earnestly advocated their cause, and that among these were actually the majority of the journalists. To those who did not understand American politics in detail, the spectacle of about one-third of the population, even though backed by constitutional law, opposing the majority, seemed to call for little sympathy. And if the motto of Emancipation for the sake of the white man offended the American Abolitionists, who were unable to see that it was a *ruse de guerre* in their favour, it is not remarkable that the English Abolitionists should have been equally obtuse.

A much more serious trouble than that of European indifference soon arose in the negro question. There were in the rebel states nearly 4,000,000 slaves. In Mr. Lincoln's party, the Republican, were two classes of men—the Abolitionists, who advocated immediate enfranchisement of all slaves by any means; and the much larger number of men who, while they were opposed to the extension of slavery, and would have liked to see it *legally* abolished, still remembered that it was constitutional. Slave property had become such a sacred thing, and had been legislated about and quarrelled over to such an extent, that, even among slavery-haters, it was a proof of honest citizenship to recognise it. Thus, for a long time after the war had begun, General M'Clellan, and many other officers like him, made it a point of returning fugitive slaves to their rebel masters. These slaves believed "the Yankees" had come to deliver them from bondage. "They were ready to act as guides, to dig, to work, to fight for liberty," and they were welcomed, on coming to help their country in its need, by being handed back to the enemy to be tortured or put to death. So great were the atrocities perpetrated in this way, and so much did certain Federal officers disgrace themselves by hunting negroes and truckling to the enemy, that a bill was soon passed in Congress, declaring it was no part of the duty of the soldiers of the United States to capture and return fugitive slaves. About the same time, General B. F. Butler, of the Federal forces, shrewdly declared that slaves were legally property, but that, as they were employed by their masters against the Government, they might be seized as *contraband of war*, which was accordingly done; nor is it recorded that any of the slaves who were by this ingenious application of law confined within the limits of freedom ever found any fault with it. From this time, during the war, slaves became popularly known as contrabands.

It should be distinctly understood that there were

now literally millions of staunch Union people, who, while recognising the evils of slavery, would not be called Abolitionists, because slavery was as yet *legal*, and according to that constitution which they properly regarded as the very life of all for which were fighting. And they would not, for the sake of removing the sufferings of the blacks, bring greater misery on the whites. Badly as the South had behaved, it was still loved, and it was felt that Abolition would bring ruin on many friends. But as the war went on, and black crape began to appear on Northern bell-handles, people began to ask one another whether it was worth while to do so much to uphold slavery, even to conciliate the wavering Border States. Step by step, arguments were found for the willing at heart but unwilling to act. On the 1st January, 1862, the writer established in Boston a political magazine, called "The Continental Monthly," the entire object of which was expressed in the phrase, *Emancipation for the sake of the white man*, and which was published solely for the sake of preparing the public mind for, and aiding in, Mr. Lincoln's peculiar policy with regard to slavery. As the writer received encouragement and direction from the President and more than one member of the Cabinet, but especially from Mr. Seward, he feels authorised, after the lapse of so many years, to speak freely on the subject. He had already, for several months, urged the same principles in another and older publication (the New York "Knickerbocker"). The "Continental" was quite as bitterly attacked by the anti-slavery press as by the pro-slavery; but it effected its purpose of aiding President Lincoln, and the editor soon had the pleasure of realising that many thousands were willing to be called Emancipationists who shrunk from being classed as Abolitionists.

In this great matter, the President moved with a caution which cannot be too highly commended. He felt and knew that the emancipation of the slaves was a great and glorious thing, not to be frittered away by the action of this or that subordinate, leaving details of its existence in every direction to call for infinite legislation. It is true that for a time he temporised with "colonisation;" and Congress passed a resolution that the United States ought to co-operate with any state which might adopt a gradual emancipation of slavery, placing 600,000 dollars at the disposition of the President for an experiment at colonisation. Some money was indeed spent in attempts to colonise slaves in Hayti, when the project was abandoned. But this was really delaying to achieve a definite purpose. On August 22nd, 1862, in reply to Horace Greeley, Mr. Lincoln wrote :—

"My paramount object is to save the Union, and not to either save or destroy slavery. If I could save the Union without freeing any slave, I would do it; if I could save it by freeing all the slaves, I would do it; and if I could do it by freeing some and leaving others alone, I would also do that. . . . I have here stated my purpose according to my views of official duty, *and I intend no modification of my oft-expressed personal wish, that all men everywhere could be free.*"

He had, meanwhile, his troubles with the army. On May 9th, 1862, General Hunter issued an order, declaring the slaves in Georgia, Florida, and South Carolina to be for ever free; which was promptly and properly repudiated by the President, who was at the time urging on Congress and the Border States a policy of gradual emancipation, with compensation to loyal masters. General Hunter's attempt at such a crisis to take the matter out of the hands of the President, was a piece of presumption which deserved severer rebuke than he received in the firm yet mild proclamation in which Lincoln, uttering no reproof, said to the General—quoting from his Message to Congress—

"I beg of you a calm and enlarged consideration of the signs of the times, ranging, if it may be, far above partisan and personal politics.

"This proposal makes common cause for a common object, casting no reproaches upon any. It acts not the Pharisee. The change it contemplates would come gently as the dews of heaven, not rending or wrecking anything. Will you not embrace it?"

General J. C. Fremont, commanding the Western

Department, which comprised Missouri and a part of Kentucky, had also issued an unauthorised order (August 31st, 1861), proclaiming martial law in Missouri, and setting the slaves, if rebels, free; which error the President at once corrected. This was taken off by a popular caricature, in which slavery was represented as a blackbird in a cage, and General Fremont as a small boy trying to let him out, while Lincoln, as a larger boy, was saying, "That's *my* bird —let him alone." To which General Fremont replying, "But you said you wanted him to be set free," the President answers, "I know; but *I'm* going to let him out—not you."

To a deputation from all the religious denominations in Chicago, urging immediate emancipation, the President replied, setting forth the present inexpediency of such a measure. But, meanwhile, he prepared a declaration that, on January 1st, 1863, the slaves in all states, or parts of states, which should then be in rebellion, would be proclaimed free. By the advice of Mr. Seward, this was withheld until it could follow a Federal victory, instead of seeming to be a measure of mere desperation. Accordingly, it was put forth—September 22nd, 1862—five days after the battle of Antietam had defeated Lee's first attempt at invading the North, and the promised proclamation was published on the 1st January following. The text of this document was as follows:—

BY THE PRESIDENT OF THE UNITED STATES OF AMERICA.

A Proclamation.

Whereas, on the twenty-second day of September, in the year of our Lord one thousand eight hundred and sixty-two, a proclamation was issued by the President of the United States, containing, among other things, the following, to wit:—

That, on the first day of January, in the year of our Lord one thousand eight hundred and sixty-three, all persons held as slaves within any state, or designated part of a state, the people whereof shall then be in rebellion against the United States, shall be then, thenceforward and for ever, free; and the Executive Government of the United States, including the naval and military authority thereof, will recognise and maintain the freedom of such persons, and will do no act or acts to repress such persons, or any of them, in any efforts they may make for their actual freedom.

That the Executive will, on the first day of January aforesaid, by proclamation, designate the states and parts of states, if any, in which the people thereof, respectively, shall then be in rebellion against the United States; and the fact that any state, or the people thereof, shall on that day be in good faith represented in the Congress of the United States, by members chosen thereto at elections wherein a majority of the qualified voters of such state shall have participated, shall, in the absence of strong countervailing testimony, be deemed conclusive evidence that such state, and the people thereof, are not then in rebellion against the United States.

Now therefore, I, Abraham Lincoln, President of the United States, by virtue of the power in me vested as commander-in-chief of the army and navy of the United

States, in time of actual armed rebellion against the authority and Government of the United States, and as a fit and necessary war-measure for suppressing said rebellion, do, on this first day of January, in the year of our Lord one thousand eight hundred and sixty-three, and in accordance with my purpose so to do, publicly proclaimed for the full period of one hundred days from the day first above-mentioned, order and designate as the states and parts of states wherein the people thereof, respectively, are this day in rebellion against the United States, the following, to wit— ARKANSAS, TEXAS, LOUISIANA (except the parishes of St. Bernard, Plaquemines, Jefferson, St. John, St. Charles, St. James, Ascension, Assumption, Terre Bonne, Lafourche, St. Mary, St. Martin, and Orleans, including the City of New Orleans), MISSISSIPPI, ALABAMA, FLORIDA, GEORGIA, SOUTH CAROLINA, NORTH CAROLINA, and VIRGINIA (except the forty-eight counties designated as West Virginia, and also the counties of Berkeley, Accomac, Northampton, Elizabeth City, York, Princess Ann, and Norfolk, including the cities of Norfolk and Portsmouth), and which excepted parts are left for the present precisely as if this proclamation were not issued.

And by virtue of the power, and for the purpose aforesaid, I do order and declare that all persons held as slaves within said designated states and parts of states are, and henceforward shall be, free; and that the Executive Government of the United States, including the military and naval authorities thereof, will recognise and maintain the freedom of said persons.

And I hereby enjoin upon the people so declared to be free, to abstain from all violence, unless in necessary self-defence; and I recommend to them that, in all cases where allowed, they labour faithfully for reasonable wages.

And I further declare and make known that such persons, of suitable condition, will be received into the armed service of the United States, to garrison forts, positions, stations, and other places, and to man vessels of all sorts in said service.

And upon this act, sincerely believed to be an act of justice warranted by the Constitution upon military necessity, I invoke the considerate judgment of mankind and the gracious favour of Almighty God.

In witness whereof I have hereunto set my hand, and caused the seal of the United States to be affixed.

L. S.   Done at the CITY OF WASHINGTON this first day of January, in the year of our Lord one thousand eight hundred and sixty-three, and of the Independence of the United States of America the eighty-seventh,

By the President,
ABRAHAM LINCOLN.
WILLIAM H. SEWARD, *Secretary of State.*

A true copy, with the autograph signatures of the President and the Secretary of State.

JOHN G. NICOLAY,
Priv. Sec. to the President.

The excitement caused by the appearance of the proclamation of September 22nd, 1862, was very great. The anti-slavery men rejoiced as at the end of a dreadful struggle; those who had doubted became at once strong and confident. Whatever trials and troubles might be in store, all felt assured, even the Copperheads or rebel sympathisers, that slavery was virtually at an end. The newspapers teemed with gratulations. The following poem, which was the first written on the proclamation, or on the day on which it appeared, and which was afterwards published in the "Continental Magazine," expresses the feeling with which it was generally received.

THE PROCLAMATION.—SEPT. 22, 1862.

Now who has done the greatest deed
   Which History has ever known?
And who in Freedom's direst need
   Became her bravest champion?
Who a whole continent set free?
   Who killed the curse and broke the ban
Which made a lie of liberty?—
   You, Father Abraham—you're the man!

The deed is done. Millions have yearned
   To see the spear of Freedom cast.
The dragon roared and writhed and burned:
   You've smote him full and square at last.
O Great and True! *you* do not know—
   You cannot tell—you cannot feel
How far through time your name must go,
Honoured by all men, high or low,
   Wherever Freedom's votaries kneel.

This wide world talks in many a tongue—
   This world boasts many a noble state;
In all your praises will be sung—
   In all the great will call you great.

> Freedom! where'er that word is known—
> On silent shore, by sounding sea,
> 'Mid millions, or in deserts lone—
> Your noble name shall ever be.
>
> The word is out, the deed is done,
> The spear is cast, dread no delay;
> When such a steed is fairly gone,
> Fate never fails to find a way.
> Hurrah! hurrah! the track is clear,
> We know your policy and plan;
> We'll stand by you through every year;
> Now, Father Abraham, you're our man.

The original draft of the proclamation of Emancipation was purchased by Thos. B. Bryan, of Chicago, for the Sanitary Commission for the Army, held at Chicago in the autumn of 1863. As it occurred to the writer that official duplicates of such an important document should exist, he suggested the idea to Mr. George H. Boker, subsequently United States Minister to Constantinople and to St. Petersburg, at whose request the President signed a number of copies, some of which were sold for the benefit of the Sanitary Fairs held in Philadelphia and Boston in 1864, while others were presented to public institutions. One of these, bearing the signatures of President Lincoln and Mr. Seward, with the attesting signature of John Nicolay, Private Secretary to the President, may be seen hanging in the George the Third Library in the British Museum. This document is termed by Mr. Carpenter, in his history of the proclamation, "the third great State paper which has marked the progress of Anglo-Saxon civilisation. First is the Magna Charta, wrested by the barons of England from King John; second, the Declaration of Independence; and third, worthy to be placed upon the tablets of history by the first two, Abraham Lincoln's Proclamation of Emancipation."

On the 7th November, Messrs. J. M. Mason and John Slidell, Confederate Commissioners to England and France, were taken from the British mail steamer *Trent* by Commodore Wilkes, of the American frigate *San Jacinto*. There was great rejoicing over this capture in America, and as great public irritation in England. War seemed imminent between the countries; but Mr. Lincoln, with characteristic sagacity, determined that so long as there was no recognition of the rebels as a nation, not to bring on a war. "One war at a time," he said. In a masterly examination of the case, Mr. Seward pointed out the fact that "the detention of the vessel, and the removal from her of the emissaries of the rebel Confederacy, was justifiable by the laws of war, and the practice and precedents of the British Government itself; but that, in assuming to decide upon the liability of these persons to capture, instead of sending them before a legal tribunal, where a regular trial could be had, Captain Wilkes had departed from the rule of international law uniformly asserted by the American Government, and forming part of its most cherished policy." The Government, therefore, cheerfully complied with the request of the British Government, and liberated the prisoners. No person at all familiar with American law or policy could doubt for an instant that this decision expressed the truth; but the adherents of the Confederacy, with their sympathisers, everywhere united in ridiculing President Lincoln for cowardice. Yet it would be difficult to find an instance of greater moral courage and simple dignity, combined with the exact fulfilment of what he thought was "just right," than Lincoln displayed on this occasion. The wild spirit of war was by this time set loose in the North, and it was felt that foreign enemies, though they might inflict temporary injury, would soon awake a principle of union and of resistance which would rather benefit than injure the country. In fact, this new difficulty was anything but intimidating, and the position of President Lincoln was for a time most embarrassing. But he could be bold enough, and sail closely enough to the law when justice demanded it. In September, 1861, the rebels in Maryland came near obtaining the passage of an act of secession in the Legislature of that state. General M'Clellan was promptly ordered to prevent this by the arrest of the treasonable legislators, which was done, and the state was saved from a civil war. Of course there was an outcry at this, as arbitrary and unconstitutional. But Governor Hicks said of it, in the Senate of the United States, "I believe that arrests, and arrests alone, saved the State of Maryland from destruction."

When Mr. Lincoln had signed the Proclamation of Emancipation, he said, "Now we have got the harpoon fairly into the monster slavery, we must take care that, in his extremity, he does not shipwreck the country." But the monster only roared. The rebel Congress passed a decree, offering freedom and reward to any slave who would kill a Federal soldier; but it is believed that none availed themselves of this chivalric offer. On the contrary, ere long there were brought into the service of the United States nearly 200,000 black troops, among whom the loss by all causes was fully one-third—a conclusive proof of their bravery and efficiency. Though the Confederates knew that their fathers had fought side by side with black men in the Revolution and at New Orleans, and though they themselves raised negro regiments in Louisiana, and employed them against the Federal Government, they were furious that such soldiers should be used against themselves, and therefore in the most inhuman manner put to death, or sold into slavery, every coloured man captured in Federal uniform.

CHAPTER IX.

Eighteen Hundred and Sixty-two—The Plan of the War, and Strength of the Armies—General M'Clellan—The General Movement, January 27th, 1862—The brilliant Western Campaign—Removal of M'Clellan—The Monitor—Battle of Fredericksburg—Vallandigham and Seymour—The Alabama—President Lincoln declines all Foreign Mediation.

THE year 1861 had been devoted rather to preparation for war than to war itself; for every day brought home to the North the certainty that the struggle would be tremendous—that large armies must fight over thousands of miles—and that to conquer, men must go forth not by thousands, but by hundreds of thousands, and endure such privations, such extremes of climate, as are little known in European warfare. But by the 1st Dec., 1861, 640,000 had been enrolled. The leading features of the plan of war were an entire blockade of the rebel coast, the military control of the border Slave States, the recovery of the Mississippi river, which is the key of the continent, and, finally, the destruction of the rebel army in Virginia, which continually threatened the North, and the conquest of Richmond, the rebel capital. General M'Clellan had in the army of the Potomac, which occupied Washington and adjacent places, more than 200,000 men, well armed and disciplined. In Kentucky, General Buell had over 100,000. The rebel force opposed to General M'Clellan was estimated at 175,000, but is now known to have been much less. General M'Clellan made little use of the spy-service, and apparently cared very little to know what was going on in the enemy's camp—an indifference which before long led him into several extraordinary and ridiculous blunders. As Commander-in-Chief, General M'Clellan had control over Halleck, Commander of the Department of the West, while General Burnside commanded in North Carolina, and Sherman in South Carolina.

But though General M'Clellan had, as he himself said, a "real army, magnificent in material, admirable in discipline, excellently equipped and armed, and well officered," and though his forces were double those of the enemy, he seemed to be possessed by a strange apathy, which, at the time, was at first taken for prudence, but which is perhaps now to be more truthfully explained by the fact that this former friend of Jefferson Davis, and ardent admirer of Southern institutions, was at heart little inclined to inflict great injury on the enemy, and was looking forward to playing the *rôle* which has led so many American politicians to their ruin—of being the great conciliator between the North and South. Through the autumn and winter of 1861–62, he did literally nothing beyond writing letters to the President, in which he gave suggestions as to the manner in which the country should be governed, and asked for more troops. All the pomp and style of a grand generalissimo were carefully observed by him; his personal camp equipage required twenty-four horses to draw it—a marvellous contrast to the rough and ready General Grant, who started on his vigorous campaign against Vicksburg with only a clean shirt and a tooth-brush. Before long, notwithstanding the very remarkable personal popularity of General M'Clellan, the country began to murmur at his slowness; and while the President was urging and imploring him to do something, the malcontents through the North began to blame the Administration for these delays. It was said to be doing all in its power to crush M'Clellan, to keep him from advancing, and to protract the war for its own political purposes.

Weary with the delay, President Lincoln (January 27th, 1862) issued a war order, to the effect that, on the 22nd February, 1862, there should be a general movement of all the land and naval forces against the enemy, and that all commanders should be held to strict responsibility for the execution of this duty. In every quarter, save that of the army of the Potomac, this was at once productive of energetic movements, hard fighting, and splendid Union victories. On the

6th November, General U. S. Grant had already taken Belmont, which was the first step in his military career, and on January 10th, Colonel Garfield defeated Humphrey Marshall at Middle Creek, Kentucky, while on January 19th, General G. H. Thomas gained a victory at Mill Spring over the rebel General Zollikoffer. The rebel positions in Tennessee and Kentucky were protected by Forts Henry and Donelson. In concert with General Grant, Commodore Foote took Fort Henry, while General Grant attacked Fort Donelson. After several days' fighting, General Buckner, in command, demanded of General Grant an armistice, in which to settle terms of surrender. To this General Grant replied, "No terms except unconditional and immediate surrender can be accepted. I propose to move immediately on your works." General Buckner, with 15,000 men, at once yielded. From this note, General U. S. Grant obtained the name of "Unconditional Surrender Grant." These successes obliged the rebels to leave Kentucky, and Tennessee was thus accessible to the Federal forces. On the 15th February, General Mitchell, of General Buell's army, reached Bowling Green, executing a march of forty miles in twenty-eight hours and a-half, performing, meanwhile, incredible feats in scaling a frozen steep pathway, a position of great strength, and in bridging a river. On the 24th February, the Union troops seized on Nashville, and on February 8th, Roanoke Island, North Carolina, with all its defences, was captured by General Burnside and Admiral Goldsborough. In March and April, Newbern, Fort Pulaski, and Fort Mason were taken from the rebels. On the 6th, 7th, and 8th of March was fought the great battle of Pea Ridge, in Arkansas, by Generals Curtis and Sigel, who had drawn General Price thither from Missouri. In this terrible and hard-contested battle the Confederates employed a large body of Indians, who, however, not only scalped and shamefully mutilated Federal troops, but also the rebels themselves. On the 7th April, General Pope took the strong position, Island No. 10, in the Mississippi, capturing with it 5000 prisoners and over 100 heavy siege guns. These great and rapid victories startled the rebels, who had been taught that the Northern foe was beneath contempt. They saw that Grant and Buell were rapidly gaining the entire south-west. They gathered together as large an army as possible, under General Albert S. Johnson and Beauregard, and the opposing forces fought, April 6th, the battle of Shiloh. Beauregard, with great sagacity, attacked General Grant with overwhelming force before Buell could come up. "The first day of the battle was in favour of the rebels, but night brought Buell, and the morrow victory, to the Union army." The shattered rebel army retreated into their strong works at Corinth, but "leaving the victors almost as badly punished as themselves." General Halleck now assumed command of the Western army, succeeding General Hunter. On the 30th May, Halleck took Corinth, capturing immense quantities of stores and a line of fortifications fifteen miles long, but was so dilatory in his attack that General Beauregard escaped, and transferred his army to aid the rebels in the East. For these magnificent victories, President Lincoln published a thanksgiving proclamation.

But while these fierce battles and great victories went on in the West, and commanders and men became alike inured to hardship and hard fighting, the splendid army of the Potomac had done nothing beyond digging endless and useless trenches, in which thousands found their graves. The tangled and wearisome correspondence which for months passed between President Lincoln and General M'Clellan is one of the most painful episodes of the war. The President urged action. General M'Clellan answered with excuses for inaction, with many calls for more men, and with repartees. At one time, when clamorous for more troops, he admitted that he had over 38,000 men absent on furlough—which accounted for his personal popularity with his soldiers. "He wrote more despatches, and General Grant fewer, than any General of the war." Meanwhile, he was building up a political party for himself in the army, and among the Northern malcontents, who thought it wrong to coerce the South. When positively ordered to march, or to seize different points, he replied with protests and plans of his own. After the battle of Antietam, September 16th, 1862, President Lincoln again urged M'Clellan to follow the retreating Confederates, and advance on Richmond. "A most extraordinary correspondence ensued, in which the President set forth with great clearness the conditions of the military problem, and the advantages that would attend a prompt movement by interior lines towards the rebel capital." In this correspondence, Lincoln displays not only the greatest patience under the most tormenting contradictions, but also shows a military genius and a clear intelligence of what should be done which indicate the greatness and versatility of his mind. He was, to the very last, kind to M'Clellan, and never seems to have suspected that the General "whose inactivity was to some extent attributable to an indisposition to inflict great injury upon the rebels," was scheming to succeed him in his office, and intriguing with rebel sympathisers. When at last the country would no longer endure the ever-writing, never-fighting General, he removed him from command (November 7th, 1862), and appointed General Burnside in his place. "This whole campaign," says Arnold, "illustrates Lincoln's patience, forbearance, fidelity to, and kindness for, M'Clellan. His misfortunes, disastrous as they were to the country, did not induce the President to abandon him. Indeed, it was a very difficult and painful thing for him ever to give up a person in misfortune, even when those misfortunes resulted from a man's own misconduct." But though he spoke kindly of General M'Clellan, Mr. Lincoln could not refrain from gently satirising the dilatory commander. Once he remarked that he would "very much like to borrow the army any day when General M'Clellan did not happen to be *using it*, to see if he could not do something with it."

On the 9th March, an incident occurred which forms the beginning of a new era in naval warfare. The rebels had taken possession of the steam frigate *Merrimac* at Norfolk, and covered her with iron armour. Sailing down the James river, she destroyed the frigates *Cumberland* and *Congress*, and was about to attack the *Minnesota*, when, by strange chance, "there came up the bay a low, turtle-like nondescript object, bearing two heavy guns, with which she attacked the *Merrimac* and saved the fleet." This was the *Monitor*, built by the celebrated engineer Ericsson.

There were many in the South, during the war, who schemed, or at least talked over, the assassination of President Lincoln. On one occasion, when he learned from a newspaper that a conspiracy of several hundred men was forming in Richmond for the purpose of taking his life, he smiled and said, "Even if true, I do not see what the rebels would gain by killing me. . . . Everything would go on just the same. Soon after I was nominated, I began to receive letters threatening my life. The first one or two made me a little uncomfortable, but I came at length to look for a regular instalment of this kind of correspondence in every week's mail. Oh! there is nothing like getting *used* to things."

General Burnside, who accepted with reluctance the command of the army (November 8th, 1862), was a manly and honourable soldier, but not more fortunate than his predecessor. Owing to a want of proper understanding and action between himself and Generals Halleck, Meigs, and Franklin, the battle of Fredericksburg, begun on the 11th December, 1862, was finally fought on the 15th January, the Union army being defeated with a loss of 12,000 men. The spirit of insubordination, of delay, and of ill-fortune which attended M'Clellan, seemed to have descended as a heritage on the army of the Potomac.

On May 3rd, 1861, President Lincoln had, in an order addressed to the Commander of the Forces on the Florida coast, suspended the writ of *habeas corpus*. The right to do so was given him by the Constitution; and in time of war, when the very foundations of society and life itself are threatened, common sense dictates that spies, traitors, and enemies may be imprisoned by military power. *Inter arma silent leges*—law must yield in war. But that large party in the North, which did not believe that anything was legal which coerced the Confederacy, was furious. On the 27th May, 1861, General Cadwalader, by the authority of the President, refused to obey a writ issued by Judge Taney—"the Judge who pronounced the Dred-Scott decision, the greatest crime in the judicial annals of the Republic"—for the release of a rebel prisoner in Fort M'Henry. The Chief Justice declared that the President could not suspend the writ, which was a virtual declaration that it was illegal to put a stop to the proceedings of the thousands of traitors in the North, many of whom, like the Mayor of New York, were in high office. In July, 1862, Attorney-General Black declared that the President had the right to arrest aiders of the rebellion, and to suspend the writ of *habeas corpus* in such cases. It was by virtue of this suspension that the rebel legislators of Maryland had been arrested, and the secession of the state prevented (September 16th, 1862). The newspapers opposed to Mr. Lincoln attacked the suspension of the writ with great fierceness. But such attacks never ruffled the President. On one occasion, when the Copperhead press was more stormy than usual, he said it reminded him of two newly-arrived Irish emigrants who one night were terribly alarmed by a grand chorus of bull-frogs. They advanced to discover the "inimy," but could not find him, until at last one exclaimed, "And sure, Jamie, I belave it's just nothing but a *naise*" (noise). Arrests continued to be made; among them was that of Clement L. Vallandigham, a member of Congress from Ohio, who, in a political canvass of his district, bitterly abused the Administration, and called on his leaders to resist the execution of the law ordering the arrest of persons aiding the enemy. For this he was properly arrested by General Burnside (May 4th, 1863), and, having been tried, was sentenced to imprisonment; but President Lincoln modified his sentence by directing that he should be sent within the rebel lines, and not be allowed to return to the United States till after the close of the war. This trial and sentence created great excitement, and by many Vallandigham was regarded as a martyr. A large meeting of these rebel sympathisers was held in Albany, at which Seymour, the Governor of New York, presided, when the conduct of President Lincoln was denounced as establishing military *despotism*. At this meeting, the Democratic or Copperhead party of New York, while nominally professing a desire to preserve the Union, took the most effectual means to destroy it by condemning the right of the President to punish its enemies. These resolutions having been sent to President

Lincoln, he replied by a letter in which he discussed at length, and in a clear and forcible style, the constitutional provision for suspension of the writ, and its application to the circumstances then existing. Many such meetings were held, condemning the Emancipation Proclamation and the sentence of Vallandigham. Great complaint was made that the President did not act on his own responsibility in these arrests, but left them to the discretion of military commanders. In answer, the President issued a proclamation meeting the objections. At the next state election, Mr. Vallandigham was the Democratic candidate for Governor, but was defeated by a majority of 100,000.

The year 1862 did not, any more than 1861, pass without foreign difficulties. Mr. Adams, the American minister in London, had remonstrated with the British Government to stop the fitting out of rebel privateers in English ports. These cruisers, chief among which were the *Alabama, Florida,* and *Georgia,* avoiding armed ships, devoted themselves to robbing and destroying defenceless merchantmen. The *Alabama* was commanded by a Captain Semmes, who, while in the service of the United States, had written a book in which he vigorously attacked, as wicked and piratical, the system of privateering, being one of the first to oppose that which he afterwards practised. Three weeks before the "290," afterwards the *Alabama,* escaped from the yard of the Messrs. Laird at Birkenhead (July, 1862), the British Government was notified of the character of the vessel, and warned that it would be held responsible for whatever damage it might inflict on American commerce. The *Alabama*, however, escaped, the result being incalculable mischief, which again bore evil fruit in later days.

In the same year the Emperor of the French made an offer of mediation between the Federal and Confederate Governments, intimating that separation was "an extreme which could no longer be avoided." The President, in an able reply (February 6th, 1863), pointed out the great recaptures of territory from the Confederates which had taken place—that what remained was held in close blockade, and very properly rejected the proposition that the United States should confer on terms of equality with armed rebels. He also showed that several of the states which had rebelled had already returned to the Union. This despatch put an end to all proposals of foreign intervention, and was of great use in clearly setting forth to the partisans of the Union the unflinching and determined character of their Government, and of the man who was its Executive head.

CHAPTER X.

Eighteen Hundred and Sixty-three—A Popular Prophecy—Gen. Burnside relieved and Gen. Hooker appointed—Battle of Chancellorsville—The Rebels invade Pennsylvania—Battle of Gettysburg—Lincoln's Speech at Gettysburg—Grant takes Vicksburg—Port Hudson—Battle of Chattanooga—New York Riots—The French in Mexico—Troubles in Missouri.

THERE was, during the rebellion, a popular rhyme declaring that "In Sixty-one, the war begun; in Sixty-two, we'll put it through; in Sixty-three, the nigger 'll be free; in Sixty-four, the war 'll be o'er—and Johnny come marching home." The predictions were substantially fulfilled. On January 1st, 1863, nearly 4,000,000 slaves who had been merchandise became men in the sight of the law, and the war, having been literally "put through" with great energy, was beginning to promise a definite success to the Federal cause. But the Union owed this advance less to its own energy than to the great-hearted, patient, and honest man who was at its head, and who was more for his country and less for himself than any one who had ever before waded through the mud of politics to so high a position. That so tender-hearted a man should have been so firm in great trials, is the more remarkable when we remember that his gentleness often interfered with justice. When the rebels, by their atrocities to the black soldiers who fell into their hands, caused him to issue an order (July 30th, 1863), declaring that "for every soldier of the United States killed in violation of the laws of war a rebel soldier shall be executed, and for every one sold into slavery a rebel soldier shall be placed at hard labour," it seemed as if vigorous retaliation was at last to be inflicted. "But," as Ripley and Dana state, "Mr. Lincoln's natural tender-heartedness prevented him from ever ordering such an execution."

Lincoln having discovered in the case of M'Clellan that incompetent or unlucky generals could be "relieved" without endangering the country, General Burnside, after the disaster of Fredericksburg, was set aside (January 24th, 1863), and General Joseph Hooker appointed in his place to command the army of the Potomac. From the 27th of April, General Hooker advanced to Kelly's Ford, and thence to Chancellorsville. A force under General Stoneman had succeeded in cutting the railroad in the rear of the rebels, so as to prevent their receiving reinforcements from Richmond, General Hooker intending to attack them flank and rear. On the 2nd May, he met the enemy at Chancellorsville, where, after a terrible battle, which continued with varying success for three days, he was compelled to withdraw his army to the north bank of the Rappahannock, having lost nearly 18,000 men. The rebel loss was also very large. General Stonewall Jackson was killed through an accidental shot from one of his own men. Inspired by this success, the Confederate General Lee resolved to move into the enemy's country. On the 9th June, he advanced north-west to the valley of the Shenandoah. On the 13th, the rebel General Ewell, with a superior force, attacked and utterly defeated General Milroy at Winchester. On the 14th July, the rebel army marched into Maryland, with the intention of invading Pennsylvania. A great excitement sprung up in the North. In a few days the President issued a proclamation, calling for 120,000 troops from the states most in danger. They were promptly sent, and, in addition to these, thousands formed themselves into improvised companies and hurried off to battle—for in those days almost every man, at one time or another, had a turn at the war, the writer himself being one of those who went out in this emergency. The danger was indeed great, and had Lee been the Napoleon which his friends thought him, he might well enough have advanced to Philadelphia. That on one occasion three of his scouts came within sight of Harrisburg I am certain, having seen them with my own eyes, though no one then deemed it credible. But two years after, when I mentioned it to a wounded Confederate Colonel who had come in to receive parole in West

Virginia, he laughed, and assured me that, on the day of which I spoke, three of his men returned, boasting that they had been in sight of Harrisburg, but that, till he heard my story, he had never believed them. And this was confirmed by another Confederate officer who was with him. On the evening of that day on which I saw the scouts, there was a small skirmish at Sporting Hill, six miles south of Harrisburg, in which two guns from the artillery company to which I belonged took part, and this was, I believe, the only fighting which took place so far north during the war.

And now there came on the great battle of Gettysburg, which proved to be the turning-point of the whole conflict between North and South. For our army, as soon as the rebels advanced north, advanced with them, and when they reached Hagerstown, Maryland, the Federal headquarters were at Frederick City, our whole force, as Raymond states, being thus interposed between the rebels and Baltimore and Washington. On that day, General Hooker was relieved from command of the army, and General Meade appointed in his place. This was a true-hearted, loyal soldier and gallant gentleman, but by no means hating the rebels so much at heart as to wish to "improve them all away from the face of the earth," as General Birney and others of the sterner sort would have gladly done. General Meade at once marched towards Harrisburg, upon which the enemy was also advancing. On the 1st July, Generals Howard and Reynolds engaged the Confederates near Gettysburg, but the foe being strongly posted, and superior in numbers, compelled General Howard to fall back to Cemetery Hill, around which all the corps of the Union army soon gathered. About three o'clock, July 2nd, the rebels came down in terrible force and with great fury upon the 3rd Corps, commanded by General Sickles, who soon had his leg shot off. As the corps seemed lost, General Birney, who succeeded him, was urged to fall back, but he, as one who knew no fear—being a grim fanatic—held his ground with the most desperate bravery till reinforced by the 1st and 6th Corps. The roar of the cannon in this battle was like the sound of a hundred thunderstorms, when, at one o'clock on the 3rd July, the enemy opened an artillery fire on us from 150 guns for two hours, we replying with 100; and I have been assured that, on this occasion, the wild rabbits, losing all fear of man in their greater terror at this horrid noise, ran for shelter, and leaped into the bosoms of the gunners. Now the battle raged terribly, as it did the day before, when General Wadsworth, of New York, went into fight with nearly 2000 men and came out with 700. Hancock was badly wounded. The rebels fought up to the muzzles of our guns, and killed the artillery horses, as many can well remember. And the fight was hand-to-hand when Sedgwick came up with his New Yorkers, who, though they had marched thirty-two miles in seventeen hours, dashed in desperately, hurrahing as if it were the greatest frolic in the world. And this turned the fight. The rebel Ewell now attacked the right, which had been weakened to support the centre, and the fighting became terrible; but the 1st and 6th again came to the rescue, and drove them back, leaving great heaps of dead. Of all the soldiers, I ever found these New Yorkers the most courteous in camp and the gayest under privations or in battle. On the 4th July, General Slocum made an attack at daybreak on Ewell, who commanded Stonewall Jackson's men, but Ewell, after a desperate resistance, was at length beaten.

The victory was complete, but terrible. On the Union side were 23,000 killed, wounded, and missing, and the losses of the rebels were even greater, General Lee leaving in our hands 13,621 prisoners. Lee was crushed, but General Meade, in the words of Arnold, "made no vigorous pursuit. Had Sheridan or Grant commanded in place of Meade, Lee's army would never have recrossed the Potomac." It is said that President Lincoln was greatly grieved at this oversight, and once, when asked if at any time the war might have been sooner terminated by better management, he replied, "Yes, at Malvern Hill, where

M'Clellan failed to command an immediate advance upon Richmond; at Chancellorsville, when Hooker failed to reinforce Sedgwick; and at Gettysburg, when Meade failed to attack Lee in his retreat at the bend of the Potomac."

It is said that General Meade did not know, until long after Lee had crossed (July 14th, 1863), or late in the morning, that he had done so. Now I knew, as did all with me, at two o'clock the day before (July 13th), when General Lee would cross. We knew that we could not borrow an axe from any country house, because the rebels had taken them all to make their bridge with; for I myself went to several for an axe, and could not get one. During the night, I was awake on guard within a mile or very little more of the crossing, and could hear the thunder and rattle of the rebel ambulances and caissons in headlong haste, and the groans of the wounded, to whom the rebels gave little care. If General Meade knew nothing of all this, there were hundreds in his army who did. But the truth is, that as General Meade was one who would never strike a man when he was down, so, in the entire chivalry of his nature, he would not pursue a flying and conquered foe. This was to be expected from one who was the Sidney of our war, and yet it was but mistaken policy for an enemy which wore ornaments made of the bones of Federal soldiers, whose women abused prisoners, and whose programme, published before the war began, advocated the shooting of pickets. Such a foe requires a Cromwell, and in Grant they got him.

During this summer of 1863, a part of the battlefield was bought by the State of Pennsylvania, and kept for a burial-ground for those who had fallen in the fight. On November 19th, 1863, it was duly consecrated with solemn ceremonies, on which occasion President Lincoln made a brief address, which has been thought, perhaps not without reason, to be the finest ever delivered on such an occasion.

"Four score and seven years ago our fathers brought forth upon this continent a new nation conceived in liberty, and dedicated to the proposition that all men are created equal. Now we are engaged in a great civil war, testing whether that nation, or any nation so conceived and so dedicated, can long endure. We are met on a great battlefield of that war. We have come to dedicate a portion of that field as a final resting-place for those who here gave their lives that the nation might live. It is altogether fitting and proper that we should do this. But in a larger sense we cannot dedicate—we cannot consecrate—we cannot hallow this ground. The brave men, living and dead, who struggled here, have consecrated it far above our power to add or detract. The world will little note, nor long remember, what we say here, but it can never forget what they did here. It is for us, the living, rather to be dedicated here to the unfinished work which they who fought here have thus so far nobly advanced. It is rather for us to be here dedicated to the great task remaining before us—that from these honoured dead we take increased devotion to the cause for which they here gave the last full measure of devotion—that we here highly resolve that the dead shall not have died in vain—that the nation shall, under God, have a new birth of freedom—and that the Government of the people, by the people, and for the people, shall not perish from the earth."

These simple yet grand words greatly moved his hearers, and among the thousands could be heard sobs and broken cheers. On this occasion, Edward Everett, "New England's most polished and graceful orator," also spoke. And this was the difference between them—that while Everett made those present think only of him living in their admiration of his art, the listeners forgot Lincoln, and wept in thinking of the dead. But it is to Mr. Everett's credit that on this occasion, speaking to the President, he said, "Ah! Mr. Lincoln, how gladly would I exchange all my hundred pages to have been the author of your twenty lines."

Meanwhile, the army of the West had been far from idle. The great Mississippi, whose arms reach to sixteen states, was held by the rebels, who thus imprisoned the North-West. Those who ask why the Confederacy was not allowed to withdraw in peace, need only look at the map of North America for an answer. And to President Lincoln belongs specially the credit of having planned the great campaign which freed the Mississippi. He was constantly busy with it; "his room," says Arnold, "was ever full of maps and plans; he marked upon them every movement, and no subordinate was at all times so completely a master of the situation." He soon appreciated the admirable qualities of the unflinching Grant, and determined that he should lead this decisive campaign in the West. General Grant had many enemies, and some of them accused him of habits of intemperance. To one of these, endeavouring to thus injure the credit of the General, President Lincoln said, "*Does* Grant get drunk?" "They say so," was the reply. "Are you *quite* sure he gets drunk?" "Quite." There was a pause, which the President broke by gravely exclaiming, "I wonder where he buys his whiskey!" "And why do you want to know?" was the astonished answer. "Because if I did," replied Mr. Lincoln, "I'd send a barrel or two of it round to some other Generals I know of."

In January, 1863, Generals M'Clernand and Sherman, commanding the army of the Mississippi, acting with the fleet under command of Admiral Porter, captured Arkansas Post, with 7000 prisoners and many cannon. On the 2nd February, General Grant arrived near Vicksburg. His object was to get his army below and behind this city, and the difficulties in the way were enormous, as the whole vicinity of the place "was a network of bayous, lakes, marshes, and old channels of streams." For weeks the untiring Grant was baffled in his efforts to cut a channel or find a passage, so as to approach the city from the ridge in the rear. He was, as Washburne said, "terribly in earnest." He had neither horse, nor servant, nor camp chest, nor for days even a blanket. He fared like the commonest soldier under his command, partaking the same rations, and sleeping on the ground under the stars. After many failures, the General, "with a persistence which has marked his whole career, conceived a plan without parallel in military history for its boldness and daring." This was briefly to march his army to a point below Vicksburg, "then to run the bristling batteries of that rebel Gibraltar, exposed to its hundreds of heavy guns, with his transports, and then to cross the Mississippi below Vicksburg, and, returning, attack that city in the rear." The crews of the very frail Mississippi steamboats, aware of the danger, with one exception, refused to go. But when Grant called for volunteers, there came from his army such numbers of pilots, engineers, firemen, and deck-hands, that he had to select by lot those who were to sail on this forlorn hope. And they pressed into the desperate undertaking with such earnestness, that great numbers offered all their money for a chance in this lottery of death, as much as 100 dollars in

United States currency being offered and refused by those who had had the luck to get what seemed to be a certainty to lose their lives. And these men truly rode into the jaws of death, believing long beforehand that there was very little hope for any one to live. Into the night they sailed in dead silence, and then, abreast of the city, there came from the batteries such a blaze of fire and such a roar of artillery as had seldom been seen or heard in the war. The gunboats fired directly on the city; the transports went on at full speed, and the troops were landed. But this was only the first step in a tremendous drama. The battle at the taking of Fort Gibson was the next. Now Grant found himself in the enemy's country, between two fortified cities, with two armies, greatly his superior in numbers, against him. Then followed battle after battle, and "rapid marches, brilliant with gallant charges and deeds of heroic valour, winning victories in quick succession—at Raymond on the 12th, at Jackson the capital of Mississippi on the 14th, at Baker's Creek on the 16th, at Big Block River on the 17th, and finally closing with driving the enemy into Vicksburg, and completely investing the city." The whole South was in terror, and Jefferson Davis sent messages far and wide, imploring every rebel to hasten to Vicksburg. It was all in vain. After desperately assaulting the city without success, Grant resolved on a regular siege. "Then, with tireless energy, with sleepless vigilance night and day, with battery and rifle, with trench and mine, the army made its approaches, until the enemy, worn out with fatigue, exhausted of food and ammunition, and driven to despair, finally laid down their arms," Grant sternly refusing, as was his wont, any terms to the conquered. By this capture, with its accompanying engagements, the rebels lost 37,000 prisoners and 10,000 killed and wounded. The joy which this victory excited all through the Union was beyond description. President Lincoln wrote to General Grant a letter which was creditable to his heart. In it he frankly confessed that Grant had understood certain details better than himself. "I wish to make personal acknowledgment," he said, "that you were right and I was wrong."

In this war the rebels set the example of greatly encouraging irregular cavalry and guerillas, having always an idea that the Northern army would be exterminated in detail by sharp-shooters, and cut to pieces with bowie-knives. This, more than any other cause, led to their own ruin, for all such troops in a short time became mere brigands, preying on friends as well as foes. On both sides there were dashing raids, and at first the rebels, having better cavalry, had the best of it. But as the war went on, there were great changes. Cavalry soldiers from horses often came to mules, or even down to their own legs; while infantry, learning that riding was easier than walking, and horse-stealing as easy as either, transformed themselves into cavalry, without reporting the change to the general in command, and if they had done so, the chances are ten to one he and all his staff would have been found mounted on just such unpaid-for steeds. If the rebels Ashley, Morgan, and Stewart set fine examples in raiding, they were soon outdone by Phil Sheridan and Kilpatrick—who was as good an orator as soldier, and who once, when surprised by the rebels, fought and won a battle in his shirt—or Custer and Grierson, Dahlgren and Pleasanton. Of this raiding and robbing it may be truly said that, while the South taught the trick, it did, after all, but nibble at the edges of the Northern cake, while the Federals sliced theirs straight through.

General Banks, who had succeeded General Butler in the Department of the Gulf, invested Port Hudson. The siege lasted until May 8th, and during the attack, the black soldiers, who had been slaves, fought with desperate courage, showing no fear whatever. In America we had been so accustomed to deny all manliness to the negro, that few believed him capable of fighting, though many thought otherwise near Nashville in 1864, when they saw whole platoons of black soldiers lying dead in regular rows, just as they had been shot down facing the enemy. Even the common soldiers opposed the use of black troops, until the idea rose slowly on their minds that a negro was not only as easy to hit as a white man, but much more likely to attract a bullet from the chivalry. As I once heard a soldier say, "I used to be opposed to having black troops, but yesterday, when I saw ten cart-loads of dead niggers carried off the field, I thought it better they should be killed than I." Of this tender philanthropy, which was willing to let the negro buy a place in the social scale at the expense of his life, there was a great deal in the army, especially among the Union-men of the South-West, who, while brave as lions or grizzly bears, were yet prudent as prairie-dogs, as all true soldiers should be. This charge of the Black Regiment at Port Hudson was made the subject of a poem by George H. Boker, which became known all over the country.

> "Now," the flag-sergeant cried,
> "Though death and hell betide,
> Let the whole nation see
> If we are fit to be
> Free in this land; or bound
> Down, like the whining hound—
> Bound with red stripes of pain
> In our old chains again!"
> Oh, what a shout there went
> From the Black Regiment!

"Freedom!" their battle-cry—
"Freedom! or leave to die!"
Ah! and *they meant* the word
Not as with us 'tis heard.
Not a mere party shout,
They gave their spirits out;
Trusted the end to God,
And on the gory sod
Rolled in triumphant blood.
Glad to strike one free blow,
Whether for weal or woe;
Glad to breathe one free breath,
Though on the lips of death.
This was what "Freedom" lent
To the Black Regiment.

Hundreds on hundreds fell;
But they are resting well;
Scourges and shackles strong
Never shall do them wrong.
Oh, to the living few,
Soldiers, be just and true;
Hail them as comrades tried,
Fight with them side by side;
Never, in field or tent,
Scorn the Black Regiment.

On the 9th July, Port Hudson surrendered to General Banks, yielding over 5000 prisoners and fifty pieces of artillery. And now, from the land of snow to the land of flowers, the whole length of the Mississippi was once more beneath the old flag, and *free*.

Meanwhile, there was hard fighting in Tennessee. After a battle at Murfreesboro', and the seizure of that place, the Union General Rosencranz (January 5th, 1863) remained quiet, till, in June, he compelled General Bragg to retreat across the Cumberland Mountains to Chattanooga. By skilful management, he compelled the Confederates to evacuate this town. They had thus been skilfully drawn from East Tennessee, which was occupied by General Burnside. Both Rosencranz and the rebel Bragg were now largely reinforced, the former by General Hooker. At Vicksburg, Grant had taken 37,000 prisoners, which he had set free on parole, on condition that they should not fight again during the war; but these men were promptly sent to reinforce Bragg. September 19, these opposing forces began the battle of Chicamauga, in which the Union troops achieved a dearly-bought victory, though the enemy retreated by night. The Federal loss was 16,351 killed, wounded, and missing; that of the rebels, as stated in their return, was 18,000. .

October 19th, 1863, General Grant assumed full command of the Departments of Tennessee, the Cumberland, and Ohio, Thomas holding under him the first, and Sherman the second. After the desperate battle of Chicamauga, Thomas followed Rosencranz to Chattanooga, and the rebels invested the place. In October, Rosencranz was relieved.

Grant arrived on the 18th, and found the enemy occupying the steep and rocky Missionary Ridge and Lookout Mountain, on whose summit they sat like eagles. Grant had under him General Thomas, the invincible Sheridan, Hooker—who, as a hard-fighting corps-commander, was without an equal—Howard, and Blair. This battle of Chattanooga, in which the Union army charged with irresistible strength, and the storming of Lookout Mountain, formed, as has been said, the most dramatic scene of the war. There was desperate fighting above the clouds, and advancing through the mist, made denser by the smoke of thousands of guns. The Union loss in this battle was 5286 killed and wounded, and 330 missing; that of the Confederates about the same, but losing in prisoners 6242, with forty cannon. Thus Tennessee was entirely taken, in gratitude for which President Lincoln issued a proclamation, appointing a day of thanksgiving for this great victory.

In the July of this year, John Morgan, the guerilla, made a raid, with 4000 men, into Ohio—not to fight, but to rob, burn, and murder. He did much damage; but before he could recross the river, his men were utterly routed, and the pious Colonel Shackelford announced in a despatch, "By the blessing of Almighty God, I have succeeded in capturing General John Morgan, Colonel Chike, and the remainder of the command." President Lincoln, when informed soon after of the death of this cruel brigand, said, "Well, I wouldn't crow over anybody's death, but I can take this as resignedly as any dispensation of Providence."

A draft for militia had been ordered (March 3rd, 1863), and passed with little trouble, save in New York, where an immense number of the dangerous classes and foreigners of the lowest order, headed by such demagogues as Fernando Wood, sympathised with the South, and controlled the elections. There was a wise and benevolent clause in this draft, which exempted from conscription any one who would pay to Government 300 dollars. The practical result of this clause was that plenty of volunteers were always ready to go for this sum, which fixed the price of a substitute and prevented fraud; and in all the wards, the inhabitants, by making up a joint fund, were able to exempt any dweller in the ward from service, as there were always poor men enough glad to go for so much money. But in New York the mob was stirred up to believe that this was simply an exemption for the rich, and a terrible riot ensued, which was the one effort made by the Copperheads during the war to assist their Confederate friends by violence. During the four days that it lasted, the most horrible outrages were committed, chiefly upon the helpless blacks of the city, though many houses belonging to prominent Union-men were burned or sacked. As all the troops had been sent away to defend the Border and repel the rebels, there was no organised force to defend the city. After the first day the draft was forgotten, and thousands of the vilest wretches of both sexes gave themselves up simply to plunder, outrage, and murder. The mob attacked the coloured half-orphan asylum, in which nearly 800 black children were sheltered, and set fire to it, burning thirty of the children alive, and sadly abusing the rest. Insane with cruelty, they caught and killed every negro they could find. In one case, they hung a negro, and then kindled a fire under him. This riot was stirred up by rebel agents, who hoped to make a diversion in the free states in favour of their armies, and influence the elections. It did cause the weakening of the army of Meade, since many troops were promptly sent back to New York. There was also a riot in Boston, which was soon repressed. The rebels, while following out the recommendation of Jefferson Davis, had gone too far, even for his interest. He had urged pillage and incendiarism; but the Copperheads of New York found out that a mob once in motion plunders friend and foe indiscriminately. The Governor of New York, Seymour, was in a great degree responsible for all these outrages by his vigorous opposition to the draft, and by the feeble tone of his remonstrances, which suggested sympathy and encouragement for the rioters.

The arrival of troops at once put a stop to the riots.

One of the most annoying entanglements of 1863 for the Government of the United States was the presence of a French army in Mexico, ostensibly to enforce the rights of French citizens there, but in reality to establish the Archduke Maximilian as its emperor. It was given out that permanent occupation was not intended; but as it became apparent to Mr. Dayton, our Minister at Paris, that the French actually had in view a kingdom in Mexico, and as it had always been an understood principle of American diplomacy that the United States would avoid meddling in European affairs, on condition that no European Government should set up a kingdom on our continent, the position of our Administration was thus manifested—

"The United States have neither the right nor the disposition to intervene by force on either side in the lamentable war which is going on between France and Mexico. On the contrary, they practise, in regard to Mexico, in every phase of that war, the non-intervention which they require all foreign powers to observe in regard to the United States. But, notwithstanding this self-restraint, this Government knows full well that the inherent normal opinion of Mexico favours a government there, republican in its form and domestic in its organisation, in preference to any monarchical institutions to be imposed from abroad. This Government knows also that this normal opinion of the people of

Mexico resulted largely from the influence of popular opinion in this country, and is continually invigorated by it. The President believes, moreover, that this popular opinion of the United States is just in itself, and eminently essential to the progress of civilisation on the American continent, which civilisation, it believes, can and will, if left free from European resistance, work harmoniously together with advancing refinement on the other continents. . . . Nor is it necessary to practise reserve upon the point that if France should, upon due consideration, determine to adopt a policy in Mexico adverse to the American opinion and sentiments which I have described, that policy would probably scatter seeds which would be fruitful of jealousies which might ultimately ripen into collision between France and the United States and other American republics."

The French Government was anxious that the United States should recognise the Government of Maximilian, but its unfriendly and unsympathetic disposition towards the Federal Government was perfectly understood, and "the action of the Administration was approved of by the House of Representatives in a resolution of April 4th, 1864."

Eighteen hundred and sixty-three had, however, much greater political trouble, the burden of which fell almost entirely on President Lincoln. The Emancipation principles were not agreeable to the most ultra Abolitionists, who were willing at one time to let the South secede rather than be linked to slavery, and who at all times, in their impatience of what was undeniably a terrible evil, regarded nothing so much as the welfare of the slaves. Time has since shown that Emancipation, which in its broad views included the interests of both white and black, was by far the wisest for both. In Missouri, these differences of opinion were fomented by certain occurrences into painful discord among the Union-men. In 1861, General Fremont, having military command of the state, proclaimed that he assumed the administrative power, thus entirely superseding the civil rulers. General Fremont, it will be remembered, also endeavoured, by freeing the slaves, to take to himself functions belonging only to the President. He, like General M'Clellan, affected great state, and before his removal (November 2nd, 1863), was censured by the War Office for lavish and unwarranted expenditures, which was significant indeed in the most extravagantly expensive war of modern times. Fremont's removal greatly angered his friends, especially the Germans. On the other hand, General Halleck, who succeeded General Hunter—who had been *locum tenens* for only a few days after Fremont's removal—made bad worse by excluding fugitive slaves from his lines. All this was followed by dissensions between General Gamble, a gradual Emancipationist, and General Curtis, who had been placed in command (September 19th, 1863) when the states of Missouri, Kansas, and Arkansas were formed into a military district. During the summer, the Union army being withdrawn to Tennessee, Kansas and Missouri were overrun by bands of guerillas, under an infamous desperado named Colonel Quantrill, whose sole aim was robbery, murder, and outrage, and who made a speciality of burning churches. This brigand, acting under Confederate orders, thus destroyed the town of Lawrence, Kansas. For this, Government was blamed, and the dissensions grew worse. Therefore, General Curtis was removed, and General Schofield put in his place, which gave rise to so many protests, that President Lincoln, at length fairly roused, answered one of these remonstrances as follows :—

"It is very painful to me that you in Missouri can not or will not settle your factional quarrel among yourselves. I have been tormented with it beyond endurance, for months, by both sides. Neither side pays the least respect to my appeals to your reason. I am now compelled to take hold of the case.

"A. LINCOLN."

These unreasonable quarrels lasted for a long time, and were finally settled by the appointment of General Rosencranz. No fault was found with General Schofield—in fact, in his first order, General Rosencranz paid a high tribute to his predecessor, for the admirable state in which he found the business of the department. So the difficulties died. In the

President's letter to General Schofield, when appointed, he had said, "If both factions, or neither, abuse you, you will probably be about right. Beware of being assailed by one and praised by the other." Judged by his own rule in this case, says Holland, the President was as nearly right as he could be, for both sides abused him thoroughly. It may be added that, having scolded him to their hearts' content, and declared him to be a copy of all the Neros, Domitians, and other monsters of antiquity, the Missouri Unionists all wheeled into line and voted unanimously for him at the next Presidential election, as if nothing had happened.

CHAPTER XI.

Proclamation of Amnesty—Lincoln's Benevolence—His Self-reliance—Progress of the Campaign—The Summer of 1864—Lincoln's Speech at Philadelphia—Suffering in the South—Raids—Sherman's March—Grant's Position—Battle of the Wilderness—Siege of Petersburg—Chambersburg—Naval Victories—Confederate Intrigues—Presidential Election—Lincoln Re-elected—Atrocious attempts of the Confederates.

THE American political year begins with the meeting of Congress, which in 1863 assembled on Monday, December 7th. On the 9th, President Lincoln sent to both Houses a message, in which he set forth the principal events of the year, as regarded the interests of the American people. The previous day he had issued a proclamation of amnesty to all those engaged in the rebellion, who "should take an oath to support, protect, and defend the Constitution of the United States and the union of the states under it, with the Acts of Congress passed during the rebellion, and the proclamations of the President concerning slaves." From this amnesty those were excepted who held high positions in the civil or military service of the rebels, or who had left similar positions in the Union to join the enemy. It also declared that whenever, in any of the rebel states, a number of persons, not less than one-tenth of the qualified voters, should take this oath and establish a state government which should be republican, it should be recognised as the government of the state. On the 24th March, he issued a proclamation following this, in which he defined more closely the cases in which rebels were to be pardoned. He allowed personal application to himself in all cases. Mr. Lincoln was of so gentle a disposition that he seldom refused to sign a pardon, and a weeping widow or orphan could always induce him to pardon even the worst malefactors. The manner in which he would mingle his humorous fancies, not only with serious business, but with almost tragic incidents, was very peculiar. Once a poor old man from Tennessee called to beg for the life of his son, who was under sentence of death for desertion. He showed his papers, and the President, taking them kindly, said he would examine them, and answer the applicant the next day. The old man, in an agony of anxiety, with tears streaming, cried, "To-morrow may be too late! My son is under sentence of death. *It must be done now, or not at all.*" The President looked sympathetically into the old man's face, took him by the hands, and pensively said, "*That* puts me in mind of a little story. Wait a bit—I'll tell it.

"Once General Fisk of Missouri was a Colonel, and he despised swearing. When he raised his regiment in Missouri, he proposed to his men that he should do all the profanity in it. They agreed, and for a long time not a solitary swear was heard among them. But there was an old teamster named John Todd, who, one day when driving his mules over a very bad road, and finding them unusually obstinate, could not restrain himself, and burst into a tremendous display of ground and lofty swearing. This was overheard by the Colonel, who at once brought John to book. 'Didn't you promise,' he said, indignantly, 'that I was to do all the swearing of the regiment?' 'Yes, I did, Colonel,' he replied; 'but the truth is, the swearing had to be done then, or not at all—and you weren't there to do it.' Well," concluded Mr. Lincoln, as he took up a pen, "it seems that this pardon has to be done now, or not at all, like Todd's swearing; and, for fear of a mistake," he added, with a kindly twinkle in his eye, "I guess we'll do it at once." Saying this, he wrote a few lines, which caused the old man to shed more tears when he read them, for the paper held the pardon of his son. Once, and once only, was President Lincoln known to sternly and promptly refuse mercy. This was to a man who had been a slave-trader, and who, after his term of imprisonment had expired, was still kept in jail for a fine of 1000 dollars. He fully acknowledged his guilt, and was very touching in his appeal on paper, but Lincoln was unmoved. "I could forgive the foulest murder for such an appeal," he said, "for it is my weakness to be too easily moved by appeals for mercy; but the man who could go to Africa, and rob her of her children, and sell them into endless bondage, with no other motive than that of getting dollars and cents, is so much worse than the most depraved murderer, that he can never receive pardon at my hands. No; he may rot in jail before be shall have liberty by any act of mine." On one occasion, when a foolish young fellow was condemned to death for not joining his regiment, his friends went with a pardon, which they begged the President to sign. They found him before a table, of which every inch was deeply covered with papers. Mr. Lincoln listened to their request, and proceeded to another table, where there was room to write. "Do you know," he said, as he held the document of life or death in his hand, "that table puts me in mind of a little story of the Patagonians. They open oysters and eat them, and throw the shells out of the window till the pile gets higher than the house, and then"— he said this, writing his signature, and handing them the paper—"*they move.*"

Holland tells us that, in a letter to him, a personal friend of the President said, "I called on him one day in the earlier part of the war. He had just written a pardon for a young man who had been sentenced to be shot for sleeping at his post as sentinel. He remarked, as he read it to me, "I could not think of going into eternity with the blood of that poor young man on my skirts." Then he added, "It is not to be wondered at that a boy raised on a farm, probably in the habit of going to bed at dark, should, when required to watch, fall asleep; and I cannot consent to shoot him for such an act." This story has a touching continuation in the fact that the dead body of this youth was found among the slain on the field of Fredericksburg, wearing next his heart a photograph of the great President, beneath which was written, *God bless President Lincoln.* Once, when a General went to Washington to urge the execution of twenty-four deserters, believing that the army was in danger from the frequency of desertion, President Lincoln replied, "General, there are already too many weeping widows in the United States. For God's sake, don't ask me to add to the number, for I won't do it."

It is certain that every man who knew anything of the inner workings of American politics, or of Cabinet secrets, during the war, will testify that no President ever did so much himself, and relied as little on others, as Lincoln. The most important matters were decided by him alone. He would listen to his Cabinet, or to anybody, and shrewdly avail himself of information or of ideas, but no human being ever had the slightest personal *influence* on him. Others might look up the decisions and precedents, or suggest the legal axioms for him, but he invariably managed the case, though with all courtesy and deference to his diplomatic junior counsel. He was brought every day into serious argument with the wisest, shrewdest, and most experienced men, both foreign and American, but his own intelligence invariably gave him the advantage. And it is not remarkable that the man who had been too much for Judge Douglas should hold his own with any one. While he was President, his wonderful powers of readily acquiring the details of any subject were thoroughly tested, and as President, he perfected the art of dealing with men. One of his French biographers, amazed at the constantly occurring proofs of his personal influence, assures his readers that, "during the war, Lincoln showed himself an organiser of the first class. A new Carnot, he created armies by land and navies by sea, raised militia, appointed generals, directed public affairs, defended them by law, and overthrew the art of maritime war by building and launching his terrible monitors. He showed himself a finished diplomatist, and protected the interests of every one. His success attested the mutual confidence of people and President in their common patriotism. The emancipation of the slaves crowned his grand policy." If some of these details appear slightly exaggerated, it must be borne in mind that all this and more appears to be literally true to any foreigner who, in studying Lincoln's life, learns what a prodigious amount of work was executed by him, and to what a degree he impressed his own mind on everything. He either made a shrewd remark or told a story with every signature to any remarkable paper, and from that day the document, the deed, and the story were all remembered in common.

On the 1st February, 1864, the President issued an order for a draft for 500,000 men, to serve for three years or during the war, and (March 14th) again for 200,000 men for service in the army and navy. On the 26th February, 1864, General Grant, in the words of the President, received "the expression of the nation's approbation for what he had done, and its reliance on him for what remained to do in the existing great struggle," by being appointed Lieutenant-General of the army of the United States.[1] It was owing to Mr. Lincoln that General Grant received the full direction of military affairs, limited by no annoying conditions. He at once entered on a vigorous course of action. "The armies of Eastern Tennessee and Virginia," says Brockett, "were heavily increased by new levies, and by an effective system of concentration; and from the Pacific to the Mississippi it soon became evident that, under the

---

[1] This honour had only been twice conferred before—once on Washington, and once by brevet on General W. Scott.—Badeau's "Life of Grant."

The Dark Summer of 1864. 179

inspiration of a great controlling mind, everything was being placed in condition for dealing a last effective blow at the already tottering Confederacy." The plan was that Sherman should take Atlanta, Georgia, and then, in succession, Savannah, Columbia, Charleston, Wilmington, and then join Grant. Thomas was to remain in the South-West to engage with Hood and Johnston, while Grant, with his Lieutenants, Meade, Sheridan, and Hancock, were to subdue General Lee and capture Richmond, the rebel capital.

But, notwithstanding the confidence of the country in General Grant, and the degree to which the Confederacy had been compressed by the victories of 1863, the summer of 1864 was the gloomiest period of the war since the dark days of 1862. In spite of all that had been done, it seemed as if the war would never end. The Croakers, whether Union-men or Copperheads,[1] made the world miserable by their complaints. And it is certain that, in the words of General Badeau, "the political and the military situation of affairs were equally grave. The rebellion had assumed proportions that transcend comparison. The Southern people seemed all swept into the current, and whatever dissent had originally existed

---

[1] Those who sympathised with the South were called Copperheads, after the deadly and treacherous snake of that name common in the Western and Southern United States.

among them, was long since, to outside apprehension, swallowed up in the maelstrom of events. The Southern snake, if scotched, was not killed, and seemed to have lost none of its vitality. In the Eastern theatre of war, no real progress had been made during three disastrous years. Gettysburg had saved Philadelphia and Washington, but even this victory had not resulted in the destruction of Lee; for in the succeeding January, the rebel chief, with undiminished legions and audacity, still lay closer to the national capital than to Richmond, and Washington was in nearly as great danger as before the first Bull Run." General Grant's first steps, though not failures, did little to encourage the North. It is true that, advancing on the 3rd of May, and fighting terribly every step from the Rapidan to the James, he "had indeed flanked Lee's army from one position after another, until he found himself, by the 1st June, before Richmond—but he had lost 100,000 men! Here the enemy stood fast at bay." The country promptly made up his immense losses; but by this time there was a vacant chair in almost every household, and the weary of waiting exclaimed every hour, "How long, O Lord! how long?"

Two things, however, were contributing at this time to cheer the North. The lavish and extravagant manner in which the Government gave out contracts to support its immense army, and the liberality with which it was fed, clothed, and paid, though utterly reprehensible from an economical point of view, had at least the good effect of stimulating manufactures and industry. In the gloomiest days of 1861-2, when landlords were glad to induce respectable tenants to occupy their houses rent-free, and poverty stared us all in the face, the writer had predicted, in the "Knickerbocker" and "Continental" Magazines, that, in a short time, the war would bring to the manufacturing North such a period of prosperity as it had never experienced, while in the South there would be a corresponding wretchedness. The prediction, which was laughed at, was fulfilled to the letter. Before the end of the war, there was a blue army coat not only on every soldier, but on almost every other man in America, for the rebels clad themselves from our battle-fields, and, in some mysterious manner, immense quantities of army stores found their way into civilian hands. All over the country there was heard not only the busy hum of factories, but the sound of the hammer, as new buildings were added to them. Paper-money was abundant, and speculation ran riot. All this made a grievous debt; but it is certain that the country got its money's worth in confidence and prosperity. When, however, despite this, people began to be downcast, certain clergymen, with all the women, organised on an immense scale a Sanitary

Commission, the object of which was to contribute comforts to the soldiers in the field. To aid this benevolent scheme, enormous "Sanitary Fairs" were held in the large cities, and these were carried out in such a way that everybody was induced to contribute money or personal exertions in their aid. These fairs, in mere magnitude, were almost like the colossal *Expositions* with which the world has become familiar, but were more varied as regards entertainment. That of Philadelphia was the Great Central Sanitary Fair, where Mr. Lincoln and his wife were present, on the 16th of June, 1864. Here I saw Mr. Lincoln for the first time. The impression which he made on me was that of an American who is reverting to the Red Indian type—a very common thing, indeed, in the South-West among pure-blooded whites. His brown complexion and high cheek-bones were very Indian. And, like the Indian chiefs, he soon proved that he had the gift of oratory when he addressed the multitude in these words—

"I suppose that this toast is intended to open the way for me to say something. War at the best is terrible, and this of ours, in its magnitude and duration, is one of the most terrible the world has ever known. It has destroyed property, destroyed life, and ruined homes. It has produced a national debt and a taxation unprecedented in the history of the country. It has caused mourning among us until the heavens may almost be said to be hung in black.

And yet it continues. It has had accompaniments not before known in the history of the world—I mean the Sanitary and Christian Commissions with their labours for the relief of the soldiers, and these fairs, first begun at Chicago, and next held in Boston, Cincinnati, and other cities. The motives and objects that lie at the bottom of them are worthy of the most that we can do for the soldier who goes to fight the battles of his country. From the tender hand of woman, very much is done for the soldier, continually reminding him of the care and thought for him at home. The knowledge that he is not forgotten is grateful to his heart. Another view of these institutions is worthy of thought. They are voluntary contributions, giving proof that the national resources are not at all exhausted, and that the national patriotism will sustain us through all. It is a pertinent question, When is this war to end? I do not wish to name a day when it will end, lest the end should not come at any given time. We accepted this war, and did not begin it. We accepted it for an object, and when that object is accomplished, the war will end; and I hope to God that it never will end until that object is accomplished. Speaking of the present campaign, General Grant is reported to have said, 'I am going to fight it out on this line if it takes all summer.' This war has taken three years; it was begun, or accepted, upon the line of restoring the national authority over the whole national domain; and for the American people, as far as my knowledge enables me to speak, I say we are going through on this line if it takes three years more. I have not been in the habit of making predictions in regard to the war, but now I am almost tempted to hazard one. I will. It is that Grant is this evening in a position, with Meade, and Hancock of Pennsylvania, whence he can never be dislodged by the enemy until Richmond is taken. If I shall discover that General Grant may be greatly facilitated in the capture of Richmond by briefly pouring to him a large number of armed men at the briefest notice, will you go? (Cries of "Yes.") Will you march on with him? (Cries of "Yes, yes.") Then I shall call upon you when it is necessary. Stand ready, for I am waiting for the chance."

The hint given in this speech was better understood when, during the next month, a call was made for 500,000 more men. These Sanitary Fairs, and the presence of Mr. Lincoln, greatly revived the spirits of the Union party. They had learned by this time that their leader was not the vulgar Boor, Ape, or Gorilla which the Southern and Democratic press persisted to the last in calling him, but a great, kind-hearted man, whose sympathy for their sorrows was only surpassed by the genius with which he led them out of their troubles. The writer once observed of Dr. George M'Clellan, father of the General, that while no surgeon in America equalled him in coolness and daring in performing the most dangerous operations, no woman could show more pity or feeling than he would in binding up a child's cut finger; and, in like manner, Abraham Lincoln, while calmly dealing at one time with the ghastly wounds of his country, never failed to tenderly aid and pity the lesser wounds of individuals.

But if the North was at this season in sorrow, those in the South had much greater cause to be so, and they all deserved great credit for the unflinching manner in which they endured their privations. From the very beginning, they had wanted many comforts; they were soon without the necessaries of civilised life. They manufactured almost nothing, and for such goods as came in by blockade-running enormous prices were paid. The upper class, who had made the war, were dependent on their servants to a degree which is seldom equalled in Europe; and, like those ants which require ant-slaves to feed them, and to which their Richmond "sociologists" had pointed as a natural example, they began to starve as their sable attendants took unto themselves the wings of Freedom and flew away. In their army, desertion and straggling were so common, that the rebel Secretary of War reported that the effective force was not more than half the men whose names appeared on the rolls. Their paper-money depreciated to one-twentieth its nominal value. There were great failures of crops in the South; the Government made constant seizures of provisions and cattle; and as the war had been confined to their own territory, the population were harried by both friend and foe.

Events were now in progress which were destined to utterly ruin the Confederacy. These were the gigantic Northern incursions, which, whether successful or not in their strategic aims, exhausted the country, and set the slaves free by thousands. Early in February, General Gillmore's attempt to establish Union government in Florida had failed. So, too, did Sherman, proceeding from Vicksburg, and Smith, leaving Memphis, fail in their plan of effecting a junction, although the destruction which they caused in the enemy's country was enormous. In the same month, Kilpatrick made a raid upon Richmond, which was eminently successful as regarded destroying railways and canals. In March, General Banks undertook an expedition to the Red River, of which it may be briefly said that he inflicted much damage, but received more. In April, Fort Pillow, on the Mississippi, held by the Union General Boyd, was treacherously captured by the rebel General Forrest, by means of a flag of truce. After the garrison of 300 white men and 350 black soldiers, with many women and children, had formally surrendered and given up their arms, a horrible scene of indiscriminate murder ensued. A committee of investigation, ordered by Congress, reported that "men, women, and little children were deliberately shot down and hacked to pieces with sabres. Officers and men seemed to vie with each other in the devilish work. They entered the hospitals and butchered the sick. Men were nailed by their hands to the floors and sides of buildings, and then the buildings set on fire." Some negroes escaped by feigning death, and by digging out from the thin covering of earth thrown over them for burial. The rebel press exulted over these barbarities, pleading the terrible irritation which the South felt at finding her own slaves armed against her. Investigation proved that this horrible massacre was in pursuance of a pre-conceived policy, which had been deliberately adopted in the hope of frightening out of the Union service not only negroes, but loyal white Southerners. From the beginning of the war, the rebels were strangely persuaded that *they* had the privilege of inflicting severities which should not be retaliated upon them. Thus at Charleston, in order to check the destructive fire of the Union guns, they placed Northern officers in chains within reach of the shells, and complacently notified our forces that they had done so. Of course an equal number of rebel officers of equal rank were at once exposed to the Confederate fire, and this step, which resulted in stopping such an inhuman means of defence, was regarded with great indignation by the South. But it was no unusual thing with rebels to kill helpless captives. A horrible instance occurred (April 20th, 1864) at the capture of Fort Plymouth, N. C., where white and black troops were murdered in cold blood after surrendering. These deeds filled the country with horror, and Mr. Lincoln, who was "deeply touched," publicly avowed retaliation, which he never inflicted.

The advance of Sherman towards the sea was not exactly what Jefferson Davis predicted (September 22nd, 1864) it would be. Sherman's force, he said, "would meet the fate of the army of the French Empire in the retreat from Moscow. Our cavalry will destroy his army . . . and the Yankee General will escape with only a body-guard." The events of this march are thus summed up by Holland. Sherman was opposed by Johnston, who, with a smaller army, had the advantage of very strong positions and a knowledge of the country, he moving towards supplies, while Sherman left his behind him. The Federal General flanked Johnston out of his works at Buzzard's Roost; and then, fighting and flanking from day to day, he drove him from Dalton to Atlanta. To do this he had to force "a difficult path through mountain defiles and across great rivers, overcoming or turning formidable entrenched positions, defended by a veteran army commanded by a cautious and skilful leader." At Atlanta, Johnston was superseded by Hood, and Hood assumed the offensive with little luck, since in three days he lost half his army, and then got behind the defences of Atlanta. Here he remained, surrounded by the toils which Sherman was weaving round him with consummate skill, and which, as Sherman admits in his admirably written report,[1] were patiently and skilfully eluded. But on the 2nd September, Atlanta fell into Sherman's hands. The aggregate loss of the Union army from Chattanooga to Atlanta was in all more than 30,000—that of the rebels above 40,000. Then Sherman proposed to destroy Atlanta and its roads, and, sending back his wounded, to move through Georgia, "smashing things to the sea." And this he did most effectually. Hood retreated to Nashville, where he was soon destined to be conquered by Thomas.

On the 12th November, Sherman began his march. The writer has heard soldiers who were in it call it a picnic. In a month he passed through to Savannah, which was held by 15,000 men; by the 20th it was taken; and on the 21st General Sherman sent to President Lincoln this despatch, "I beg to present to you as a Christmas gift the city of Savannah, with 150 guns, plenty of ammunition, and about 25,000 bales of cotton." In this march he carried away more than 10,000 horses and mules, and set free a vast number of slaves. Then, turning towards the North, the grand North-Western army co-operated with Grant, "crushing the fragments of the rebellion between the opposing forces."

Meanwhile, Hood, subdued by Sherman, had, with

---

[1] Sherman's Report, 1865; also, Report of Secretary of War, 1865.

an army of nearly 60,000 men, advanced to the North, where he was followed by General Thomas. On November 20th, Hood, engaging with Schofield, who was under Thomas, was defeated in a fierce and bloody battle at Franklin, in which he lost 6000 men. On the 15th December, the battle of Nashville took place, and lasted two days, the rebels being utterly defeated, though they fought with desperate courage. They lost more than 4000 prisoners, fifty-three pieces of artillery, and thousands of small arms.

The close of December, 1864, found the Union armies in this position—" Sheridan had defeated Early in the Shenandoah Valley; Sherman was at Savannah, organising further raids up the coast; Hood was crushed; Early's army was destroyed; Price had been routed in Missouri; Cawley was operating for the capture of Mobile; and Grant, with the grip of a bull-dog, held Lee in Richmond." The Union cause was greatly advanced, while over all the South a darkness was gathering as of despair. And yet, with indomitable pluck, they held out for many a month afterwards. And "there was discord in the councils of the rebels. They began to talk of using the negroes as soldiers. The commanding General demanded this measure; but it was too late. Lee was tied, and Sherman was turning his steps towards him, and, among the leaders of the rebellion, there was a fearful looking-out for fatal disasters." Yet, with the inevitable end full in view, the Copperhead party, now openly led by M'Clellan, continued to cry for "peace at any price," and clamour that the South should be allowed to go its way, and rule the country.

We have seen how Grant, now at the head of the entire national army of 700,000 men, had planned in council with Sherman the great Western campaign, and its result. After this arrangement, he returned to Virginia, to conduct in person a campaign against Lee. A letter which he received at this time from President Lincoln, and his answer, are equally honourable to both. That from Lincoln was as follows :—

"Executive Mansion, Washington,
"*April 30th*, 1864.

"Not expecting to see you before the spring campaign opens, I wish to express in this way my entire satisfaction with what you have done up to this time, so far as I understand it. The particulars of your plans I neither know nor seek to know. You are vigilant and self-reliant; and, pleased with this, I wish not to obtrude any restraints or constraints upon you. . . . If there be anything wanting which it is in my power to give, do not fail to let me know it. And now, with a brave army and a just cause, may God sustain you.

"A. Lincoln."

General Grant, in his reply, expressed in the most candid manner his gratitude that, from his first entrance into the service till the day on which he wrote, he had never had cause for complaint against the Administration or Secretary of War for embarrassing him in any way; that, on the contrary, he had been astonished at the readiness with which everything had been granted; and that, should he be unsuccessful, the fault would not be with the President. The manliness, honesty, and simple gratitude manifest in Grant's letter, render it one of the most interesting ever written. While M'Clellan was in command, Mr. Lincoln found it necessary to supervise; after Grant led the army, he felt that no direction was necessary, and that an iron wheel must have a smooth way. To some one inquiring curiously what General Grant intended to do, Mr. Lincoln replied, "When M'Clellan was in the hole, I used to go up the ladder and look in after him, and see what he was about; but, now this new man, Grant, has pulled up the ladder and *hauled the hole in* after him, I can't tell what he is doing."

On May 2nd, 1864, Grant marched forward, and on the next night crossed the Rapidan river. On May 5th began that terrible series of engagements known as the Battle of the Wilderness, which lasted for five days. During this conflict the Union General Wadsworth and the brave Sedgwick, the true hero of Gettysburg, were killed. Fifty-four thousand five hundred and fifty-one men were reported as killed, wounded, or missing on the Union side, from May

3rd to June 15th; Lee's losses being about 32,000. There was no decisive victory, but General Lee was obliged to gradually yield day by day, while Grant, with determined energy, flanked him until he took refuge in Richmond. At this time there was fearful excitement in the North, great hope, and greater grief, but more resolve than ever. President Lincoln was in great sorrow for such loss of life. When he saw the lines of ambulances miles in length coming towards Washington, full of wounded men, he would drive with Mrs. Lincoln along the sad procession, speaking kind words to the sufferers, and endeavouring in many ways to aid them. One day he said, "This sacrifice of life is dreadful; but the Almighty has not forsaken me nor the country, and we shall surely succeed."

Though the inflexible Grant had no idea of failure, and though his losses were promptly supplied, he was in a very critical position, where a false move would have imperilled the success of the whole war. On the 12th June, finding that nothing could be gained by directly attacking Lee, he resolved to assail his southern lines of communications. He soon reached the James river, and settled down to the siege of Petersburg.

Sherman had opened his Atlanta campaign as soon as Grant had telegraphed to him that he had crossed the Rapidan. At the same time, he had ordered Sigel to advance through the Shenandoah towards Stanton (Va.), and Crook to come up the Kanawha Valley towards Richmond, but both were defeated, while Butler, though he inflicted great damage on the enemy, instead of capturing Petersburg, was himself "sealed up," as Grant said. "All these flanking movements having failed, and Lee being neither defeated in the open field nor cut off from Richmond, the great problem of the war instantly narrowed itself down to the siege of Petersburg, which Grant began, and which, as it will be seen, long outlasted the year. Meanwhile, terrible injury was daily inflicted on the rebels in Virginia, by the numerous raiding and flanking parties which, whether conquering or conquered, destroyed everything, sweeping away villages and forests alike for firewood, as I well know, having seen miles of fences burned.

"On May 18th, just after the bloody struggle at Spottsylvania, a spurious proclamation, announcing that Grant's campaign was closed, appointing a day of fasting and humiliation, and ordering a new draft for 400,000 men, appeared in the New York 'World' and 'Journal of Commerce,' newspapers avowedly hostile to the Administration. The other journals, knowing that this was a forgery, refused to publish it. By order of the President, the offices of these two publications were closed; and, this action being denounced as an outrage on the liberty of the press,

Governor Seymour attempted to have General Dix and others indicted for it." The real authors of the forgery were two men named Howard and Mallison, their object being stock-jobbing purposes.

When General Sigel was defeated, he was relieved by General Hunter, who, at first successful, was at last obliged to retreat before the rebel Early, with very great loss. This placed Hunter in such a position that he could not protect Washington. Early, finding himself unopposed, crossed Maryland, plundered largely, fought several battles with the militia, burned private houses, destroyed the trains on the Washington and Baltimore railroads, and threatened both cities. Then there was great anxiety in the North, for just at that time Grant was in the worst of his great struggle. But when Early was within two miles of Baltimore, he was confronted by the 6th Corps from the Potomac, the 19th from Louisiana, and large forces from Pennsylvania, and driven back. During this retreat, he committed a great outrage. Having entered Chambersburg, Pennsylvania, a peaceful, unfortified town, he demanded 100,000 dollars in gold, to be paid within an hour, and as the money could not be obtained, he burned the place. Meanwhile, Sheridan had made his famous raid round Lee's lines, making great havoc with rebel stores and lines of transit, but in no manner infringing on the rules of honourable warfare.

During July, 1864, Admiral Farragut, of the Union navy, with a combination of land and sea forces, attacked Mobile. A terrible conflict ensued, resulting in the destruction of a rebel fleet, the capture of the famous armour-ship *Tennessee*, four forts, and many guns and prisoners. This victory was, however, the only one of any importance gained during this battle-summer. It effectually closed one more port. But the feeling of depression was now so great in the North, owing to the great number of deaths in so many families, that President Lincoln, by special request of the Congress—which adjourned July 4th, 1864—issued a proclamation, appointing a day of fasting and prayer. But two days after, public sorrow was "much alleviated," says Raymond, "by the news of the sinking of the pirate *Alabama*" (June 19th) by the *Kearsage*, commanded by Winslow. Yet for all the grief and gloom which existed, the Union-men of America were never so obstinately determined to resist. The temper of the time was perfectly shown in a pamphlet by Dr. C. J. Stille of Philadelphia, entitled, "How a Free People conduct a long War," which had an immense circulation, and which pointed out in a masterly manner that all wars waged by a free people for a great principle have progressed slowly and involved untiring vigour. And President Lincoln, when asked what we should do if the war should last for years, replied, "We'll keep pegging away." In short, the whole temper of the North was now that of the Duke of Wellington, when he said at Waterloo, "Hard pounding this, gentlemen; but we'll see who can pound the longest."

During the summer of 1864, two self-styled agents of the Confederate Government appeared at Clifton, Canada, in company with W. Cornell Jewett, whom Raymond terms an irresponsible and half-insane adventurer, and George Sanders, described as a political vagabond. Arnold states that expeditions to rob and plunder banks over the border, and to fire Northern cities, were subsequently clearly traced to them; "and that there is evidence tending to connect them with crimes of a still graver and darker character." These men were employed by the Confederate Government, to be acknowledged or repudiated according to the success of their efforts. They induced Horace Greeley to aid them in negotiating for peace, and he wrote to President Lincoln as follows—" I venture to remind you that our bleeding, bankrupt, almost dying country, also longs for peace; shudders at the prospect of fresh conscriptions, of further wholesale devastations, and of new rivers of human blood. I fear, Mr. President, you do not realise how intensely the people desire any peace, consistent with the national integrity and honour."

To Mr. Lincoln, who firmly believed that the best means of attaining peace was to conquer it, such language seemed out of place. Neither did he believe that these agents had any direct authority, as proved to be the case. After an embarrassing correspondence, the President sent to these "commissioners" a message, to the effect that any proposition embracing the restoration of peace, the integrity of the whole Union, and the abandonment of slavery, would be received by the Government of the United States if coming from an authority that can control the armies now at war with the United States. In answer to this, the agents declared, through Mr. Greeley, that it precluded negotiation, and revealed in the end that the purpose of their proceedings had been to influence the Presidential election. As it was, many were induced to believe that Mr. Lincoln, having had a chance to conclude an honourable peace, had neglected it.

Meanwhile, Mr. Lincoln had the cares of a Presidential campaign on his hands. Such an election, in the midst of a civil war which aroused everywhere the most intense and violent passions, was, as Arnold wrote, a fearful ordeal through which the country must pass. At a time when, of all others, confidence in their great leader was most required, all the slander of a maddened party was let loose upon him. General M'Clellan, protesting that personally he was in favour of war, became the candidate of those whose watchword was "Peace at any price," and who embraced all those who sympathised with the South and with slavery. Their "platform" was simply a treasonable libel on the Government, declaring that, "under the *pretence* of the military necessity of a war-power higher than the Constitution, the Constitution itself has been disregarded in every part, and public liberty and private rights alike trodden down, and the material prosperity of the country essentially impaired; and that justice, humanity, liberty, and the public welfare demand that immediate efforts be made for a cessation of hostilities."

It was, therefore, distinctly understood that the question at stake in this election was, whether the war should be continued. The ultra-Abolition adherents of General Fremont were willing to see a pro-slavery President elected rather than Mr. Lincoln, so great was their hatred of him and of Emancipation, and they therefore nominated their favourite, knowing that he could not be elected, but trusting to divide and ruin the Lincoln party. But this movement came to an inglorious end. A portion of the Republican party offered the nomination for the Presidency to General Grant, which that honourable soldier promptly declined in the most straightforward manner. As the election drew on, threats and rumours of revolution in the North were rife, and desperate efforts were made by Southern emissaries to create alarm and discontent. But such thorough precautions were taken by the Government, that the election was the quietest ever known, though a very heavy vote was polled. On the popular vote, Lincoln received 2,223,035; M'Clellan, 1,811,754. The latter carried only three states—New Jersey, Delaware, and Kentucky, while all the others which held an election went to Lincoln. The total number admitted and counted of electoral votes was 233, of which Lincoln and Johnson (Vice-President) had 212, and M'Clellan and Pendleton 21.

Of this election, the President said, in a speech (November 10th, 1864)—

"So long as I have been here, I have not willingly planted a thorn in any man's bosom. While I am duly sensible to the high compliment of a re-election, and duly grateful, as I trust, to Almighty God for having directed my countrymen to a right conclusion, as I think, for their good, it adds nothing to my satisfaction that any other man may be disappointed by the result. May I ask those who have not differed with me to join with me in this spirit towards those who have?"

Those who yet believe that the rebels were in the main chivalric and honourable foes, may be asked what would they have thought of the French, if, during the German war, they had sent chests of linen, surcharged with small-pox venom, into Berlin, under charge of agents officially recognised by Government? What would they have thought of

Germany, if official agents from that country had stolen into Paris and attempted to burn the city. Yet both of these things were attempted by the agents of the Confederate *Government*—not by unauthorised individuals. On one night, fires were placed in thirteen of the principal hotels of New York, while, as regards incendiarism, plots were hatched from the beginning in the South to treacherously set fire to Northern cities, to murder their public men, and otherwise make dishonourable warfare, the proof of all this being in the avowals and threats of the Southern newspapers. Immediately after the taking of Nashville by Thomas, the writer, with a friend, occupied a house in that town which had belonged to a rebel clergyman, among whose papers were found abundant proof that this reverend incendiary had been concerned in a plot to set fire to Cincinnati.

In connection with these chivalric deeds of introducing small-pox and burning hotels, must be mentioned other acts of the rebel agents, sent by their Government on "detached service." On the 19th October, a party of these "agents" made a raid into St. Albans, Vermont, where they robbed the banks, and then retreated into Canada. These men were, however, discharged by the Canadian Government; the money which they had stolen was given up to them, as Raymond states, "under circumstances which cast great suspicion upon prominent members of the Canadian Government." The indignation which this conduct excited in the United States is indescribable, and the Canadian Government, recognising their mistake, re-arrested such of the raiders as had not made their escape. But the American Government, finding that they had few friends beyond the frontier, properly established a strict system of passports for all immigrants from Canada.

The year 1864 closed under happy auspices. "The whole country had come to regard the strength of the rebellion as substantially broken." There were constant rumours of peace and reconciliation. The rebels, in their exhaustion, were presenting the most pitiable spectre of a sham government. The whole North was crowded with thousands of rebel families which would have starved at home. They were not molested; but, as I remember, they seemed to work the harder for that to injure the Government and Northern people among whom and upon whom they lived, being in this like the teredo worms, which destroy the trunk which shelters and feeds them.

CHAPTER XII.

The President's Reception of Negroes—The South opens Negotiations for Peace—Proposals—Lincoln's Second Inauguration—The Last Battle—Davis Captured—End of the War—Death of Lincoln—Public Mourning.

THE political year of 1865 began with the assemblage of Congress (December 5th, 1864). The following day, Mr. Lincoln sent in his Message. After setting forth the state of American relations with foreign Governments, he announced that the ports of Fernandina, Norfolk, and Pensacola had been opened. In 1863, a Spaniard named Arguelles, who had been guilty of stealing and selling slaves, had been handed over to the Cuban Government by President Lincoln, and for this the President had been subjected to very severe criticism. In the Message he vindicated himself, declaring that he had no doubt of the power and duty of the Executive under the law of nations to exclude enemies of the human race from an asylum in the United States. He showed an enormous increase in industry and revenue, a great expansion of population, and other indications of material progress; thus practically refuting General Fremont's shameless declaration that

Lincoln's "administration had been, politically and financially, a failure." On New Year's Day, 1865, the President, as was usual, held a reception. The negroes—who waited round the door in crowds to see their great benefactor, whom they literally worshipped as a superior being, and to whom many attributed supernatural or divine power—had never yet been admitted into the White House, except as servants. But as the crowd of white visitors diminished, a few of the most confident ventured timidly to enter the hall of reception, and, to their extreme joy and astonishment, were made welcome by the President. Then many came in. An eye-witness wrote of this scene as follows—" For nearly two hours Mr. Lincoln had been shaking the hands of the white 'sovereigns,' and had become excessively weary—but here his nerves rallied at the unwonted sight, and he welcomed this motley crowd with a heartiness that made them wild with exceeding joy. They laughed and wept, and wept and laughed, exclaiming through their blinding tears, 'God bless you!' 'God bless Abraham Lincoln!' 'God bress Massa Linkum!'"

It was usual with Louis the XI. to begin important State negotiations by means of vagabonds of no faith or credibility, that they might be easily disowned if unsuccessful; and this was precisely the course adopted by Davis and his Government when they employed Jewett and Saunders to sound Lincoln as to peace. A more reputable effort was made in February, 1865, towards the same object. On December 28th, 1864, Mr. Lincoln had furnished Secretary F. P. Blair with a pass to enter the Southern lines and return, stipulating, however, that he should in no way treat politically with the rebels. But Mr. Blair returned with a message from Jefferson Davis, in which the latter declared his willingness to enter into negotiations to secure peace to *the two countries.* To which Mr. Lincoln replied that he would be happy to receive any agent with a view to securing peace to *our common country.* On January 29th, the Federal Government received an application from A. H. Stephens, the Confederate Vice-President, R. M. T. Hunter, President of the rebel Senate, and A. J. Campbell, the rebel Secretary of War, to enter the lines as *quasi*-commissioners, to confer with the President. This was a great advance in dignity beyond Saunders and Jewett. Permission was given for the parties to hold a conference on the condition that they were not to land, which caused great annoyance to the rebel agents, who made no secret of their desire to visit Washington. They were received on board a steamboat off Fortress Monroe. By suggestion of General Grant, Mr. Lincoln was personally present at the interview. The President insisted that three conditions were indispensable—1. Restoration of the national authority in all the states; 2. Emancipation of the slaves; and 3. Disbanding of the forces hostile to Government. The Confederate Commissioners suggested that if hostilities could be suspended while the two Governments united in driving the French out of Mexico, or in a war with France, the result would be a better feeling between the South and North, and the restoration of the Union. This proposition—which, to say the least, indicated a lamentable want of gratitude to the French Emperor, who had been anxious from the beginning to recognise the South and destroy the Union, and who would have done so but for the English Government—was rejected by Mr. Lincoln as too vague. During this conference, Mr. Hunter insisted that a constitutional ruler could confer with rebels, and adduced as an instance the correspondence of Charles I. with his Parliament. To which Mr. Lincoln replied that he did not pretend to be versed in questions of history, but that he distinctly recollected that Charles I. *lost his head*. Nothing was agreed upon. But, as Mr. Stephens declared, Jefferson Davis coloured the report of this meeting so as to crush the great Southern peace-party. He began by stating that he had received a written notification which satisfied him that Mr. Lincoln wished to confer as to peace, when the truth was that Lincoln had forbidden Mr. Blair to open any such negotiation. And having, by an inflammatory report, stirred up many people to hold "black-flag" meetings and "fire the Southern heart," he said of the Northern men in a public speech—"We will teach them that, when they talk to us, they talk to their masters."[1] Or, as it was expressed by a leading Confederate journal—"A respectful attitude, *cap in hand*, is that which befits a Yankee when speaking to a Southerner."

On January 31st, the House of Representatives passed a resolution submitting to the Legislatures of all the states a constitutional amendment entirely abolishing slavery, which had already passed the Senate (April 8th, 1864). On the 4th March, 1865, Mr. Lincoln was inaugurated for a second time. Four years before, when the same ceremony was performed, he was the least known and the most hated man who had ever been made President. Since then a tremendous storm had darkened the land, and now the sky, growing blue again, let the sunlight fall on his head, and the world saw what manner of man he was. And such a day this 4th of March literally was, for it began with so great a tempest that it was supposed the address must be delivered in the Senate Chamber instead of the open air. But, as Raymond writes, "the people had gathered in

---

[1] Stephens' Statement, Augusta, Georgia, "Chronicle," June 17th, 1875. Quoted by Dr. Brockett, p. 579.

immense numbers before the Capitol, in spite of the storm, and just before noon the rain ceased, the clouds broke away, and, as the President took the oath of office, the blue sky appeared, a small white cloud, like a hovering bird, seemed to hang above his head, and the sunlight broke through the clouds, and fell upon him with a glory afterwards felt to have been an emblem of the martyr's crown which was so soon to rest upon his head." Arnold and many others declare that, at this moment, a brilliant star made its appearance in broad daylight, and the incident was regarded by many as an omen of peace. As I have myself seen in America a star at noon-day for two days in succession, I do not doubt the occurrence, though I do not remember it on this 4th of March. The inaugural address was short, but remarkable for vigour and a very conciliatory spirit. He said—

"On the occasion corresponding to this, four years ago, all thoughts were anxiously directed to an impending civil war. All dreaded it—all sought to avoid it. While the inaugural address was being delivered from this place, devoted altogether to saving the Union without war, insurgent agents were in the city seeking to destroy it without war. . . . Both parties deprecated war, but one of them would make war rather than let the nation survive, and the other would accept war rather than let it perish—and the war came. One-eighth of the population were slaves, who constituted a peculiar and powerful interest. All knew that this interest was the cause of the war. To strengthen and perpetuate this interest was the object for which the insurgents would rend the Union by war, while the Government claimed right to no more than restrict the territorial enlargement of it. . . . Both parties read the same Bible and pray to the same God, and each invokes His aid against the other. It may seem strange that any men should dare to ask a just God's assistance in wringing their bread from the sweat of other men's faces; but let us judge not that we be not judged. The prayer of both could not be answered. That of neither has been answered fully. The Almighty has His own purposes. 'Woe unto the world because of offences, for it must needs be that offences come, but woe unto the man by whom the offence cometh.' If we shall suppose that American slavery is one of these offences which, in the providence of God, must needs come, but which, having continued through His appointed time, He now wills to remove, and that He gives to both North and South this terrible war as the woe due to those by whom the offence came, shall we discern therein any departure from those Divine attributes which the believers in a living God always ascribe to Him? Fondly do we hope, fervently do we pray, that this mighty scourge of war may speedily pass away. Yet if God wills that it continue until all the wealth piled by the bondman's 250 years of unrequited toil shall be sunk, and until every drop of blood drawn with the lash shall be requited by another drawn with the sword, as was said 3000 years ago, so it must still be said the judgments of the Lord are true and righteous altogether. With malice toward no one, with charity for all, with firmness in the right as God gives us to see the right, let us strive on to finish the work we are in, to bind up the nation's wounds, to care for him who shall have borne the battle, and for his widow and his orphans, to do all which may achieve and cherish a just and lasting peace among ourselves, and with all nations."

If there was ever a sincere utterance on earth expressive of deeply religious faith, in spirit and in truth, it was in this address. And at this time not only President Lincoln, but an extraordinary number of people were inspired by a deeply earnest faith and feelings which few can *now* realise. Men who had never known serious or elevated thoughts before, now became fanatical. The death of relatives in the war, the enormous outrages inflicted by the rebels on prisoners, the system of terrorism and cruelty which they advocated, had produced on the Northern mind feelings once foreign to it, and they were now resolved to go on, "in God's name, and for this cause," to the bitter end. With the feeling of duty to God and the Constitution and the Union, scores on scores of thousands of men laid down their lives on the battle-field. And it was characteristic of the South that, having from the beginning all the means at their command of cajoling, managing, and ruling the North, as easily as ever a shepherd managed sheep, they, with most exemplary arrogance, took precisely the course to provoke all its resistance. Soldiers who had not these earnest feelings generally turned into bounty-jumpers—men who took the premium for enlisting, and deserted to enlist again—or else into marauders or stragglers. But the great mass were animated by firm enthusiasm. I have been in several countries during wild times, and have seen in a French revolution courage amounting to delirium, but never have I seen anything like the zeal which burned in every Union heart during the last two years of the war of Emancipation.

On the 6th March, 1865, Mr. Fessenden, the Secretary of the Treasury, voluntarily resigned, and Mr. Hugh M'Culloch was appointed in his place. This was the only change in the Cabinet. On the 11th March, the President issued a proclamation, pardoning all deserters from the army, on condition that they would at once return to duty. This had the effect of bringing in several thousands, who materially aided the draft for 300,000, which was begun on the 15th March, 1865.

And now the Southern Confederacy was rapidly hurrying down a darkening road to ruin—nor was it even destined to perish with honour, and true to its main principle; for, in their agony, its leaders even looked to the despised negro for help. It was proposed to the rebel Congress—and the measure was defeated by only one vote—that every negro who would fight for the Confederacy should be set free; which amounted, as Raymond declares, and as many rebels admitted, to a practical abandonment of those ideas of slavery for whose supremacy the rebellion had been set on foot. Of this proposition President Lincoln said—"I have in my life heard many arguments why the negroes ought to be slaves, but if they will fight for those who would keep them in slavery, it will be a better argument than any I have yet heard. He who would fight for that, ought to be a slave."

The beginning of the end was now approaching. Early in February, Grant advanced in person with four corps, with the object of establishing his position near the Weldon road. After several days' fighting, the Union forces were in a position four miles in advance. On the 25th March, 1865, the rebels desperately assaulted and captured Fort Stedman, a very important position near Petersburg; but the Union reserves speedily retook it. General Grant was now afraid lest Lee should escape, "and combine with Johnston, in which case a long campaign, consuming most of the summer, might become necessary."

On the 30th March, 1865, Grant attacked Lee, "with the army of the Potomac, in front, while the army of the James forced the enemy's right flank, and Sheridan, with a large cavalry force, distracting Lee's attention by a blow at the junction of the South-side, Richmond, and Danville railroads, suddenly wheeled, struck the South-side railroad within ten miles of

Petersburg, and, tearing it up as he went, fell upon the rebel left flank." During this time, and the four days which ensued, there was much resolute and brilliant strategy, desperate and rapid flanking, hard fighting, and personal heroism. It was the perfection of war, and it was well done by both adversaries. Now Petersburg was completely at the mercy of the national armies. During the tremendous cannonading of Saturday night, April 1st, 1865, Lee, in dire need, called for Longstreet to aid him. "Then," in the words of Arnold, "the bells of Richmond tolled, and the drums beat, calling militia, citizens, clerks, everybody who could carry arms, to man the lines from which Longstreet's troops were retiring." At early dawn on Sunday, April 2nd, 1865, Grant ordered a general assault along the entire line, and this, the last grand charge of the war, carried everything decisively before it. Away the rebel lines rushed in full retreat. At eleven a.m. of that eventful Sunday, Jefferson Davis, in church, received a despatch from Lee, saying Petersburg and Richmond could no longer be held. He ran in haste from church, and left the city by the Danville railroad. During the night, Richmond and Petersburg were both evacuated, the rebels first setting fire to the principal buildings in Richmond, being urged by the desperate intention of making another Moscow of their last city. The flames were, with difficulty, put out by Weitzel's cavalry. His regiment of black troops was the first to enter the stronghold of slavery, its band playing " John Brown's Body."

Lee, who had lost 18,000 prisoners and 10,000 in killed and wounded, or half his force, fled with the remainder, in the utmost disorder, toward Lynchburg. But he had not the merciful Meade in command after him this time, but a man of blood and iron, " who was determined then and there to make an end of it." " Grant's object," says Raymond, "in the whole campaign, had been, not Richmond, but Lee's army; for that he pushed forward, regardless of the captured cities which lay behind him, showing himself as relentless in pursuit as he had been undaunted in attack."[1]

President Lincoln immediately went to the front and to Richmond the day after it was taken. He entered quietly without a military guard, accompanied only by his son, Admiral Porter, and the sailors who had rowed him up. But the negroes soon found out that he was there, and came rushing, with wild cries of delight, to welcome him. This scene has been described as inexpressibly touching. The poor creatures, now knowing, for the first time, that they were really free, came, their eyes streaming with tears, weeping aloud for joy, shouting or dancing with

---

[1] It should be said that Meade, under Grant's orders, was, however, now one of Lee's most vigorous pursuers.

delight, and crying, without exception, in long chorus, "Glory, glory, glory to God!" These people, who had acquired, as it were, in an instant that freedom which they prized far above wealth, or aught else on earth, found only in religious enthusiasm vent for their feelings.

It was at Grant's suggestion that President Lincoln had so promptly visited Richmond, to which he again returned on April 6th, 1865. Meanwhile, the entire North and West was in a frenzy of delight. Those who can recall it will always speak of it as such an outburst of joyful excitement as they can hardly expect to take part in again. Cannon roared and bells were rung from the Atlantic to the Pacific; drums beat and trumpets sounded, no longer for war, but for gladness of peace. There was such gratulation and hurrahing for happiness, and such kindly greeting among strangers, that it seemed as if all the world were one family at a merry-making. And, in every family, relatives and friends began to get ready for husbands, fathers, brothers, sons, or lovers, for all knew that, in a few days, more than a million of Union soldiers would return home. For, at last, *the war was over.* The four years of sorrow and suspense were at an end.

Meanwhile, Grant was hunting Lee with headlong haste. The rebel army was cut off from its supplies and starving, its cattle falling dead, "its men falling out of the ranks by thousands, from hunger and fatigue." Fighting desperately, flanked at every turn, on April 6th, 1865, Lee was overtaken by Sheridan and Meade at Deatonville, and met with a crushing defeat. On Sunday, April 9th, 1865, he was compelled to surrender to Grant on terms which, as Arnold rightly states, were very liberal, magnanimous, and generous. The whole of Lee's army were allowed to return home on condition that they would not take up arms again against the United States—not a difficult condition for an enemy which made no scruple of immediately putting its paroled men into the field, without regard to pledge or promise, as had happened with the 37,000 Vicksburg prisoners. This stipulation gave much dissatisfaction to the Union army. On the 26th April, 1865, General Johnston surrendered his army to Sherman, not before the latter had blundered sadly in offering terms on conditions which were entirely beyond his powers to grant. Johnston finally obtained the same conditions as Lee. The other rebel forces soon yielded—General Howell Cobb surrendering to General Wilson in Georgia, on the 20th April; Dick Taylor surrendering all the forces west of the Mississippi to General Canby, to whom General Kirby Smith also surrendered on May 26th. On the 11th day of May, Jefferson Davis, flying in terror towards the sea, was captured at Irwinsville, Georgia, by the 4th Michigan Regiment. He was attired at the time as a woman, wearing his wife's waterproof cloak, and with a woman's shawl drawn over his head. Those who captured him say he was carrying a water-bucket. A rebel officer who was with him admits that he was in a loose wrapper, and that a Miss Howell fastened the shawl on to disguise him, but declares he was followed by a servant with a bucket.[1] It has been vigorously denied that Davis was thus disguised as a woman; but the affidavit of the colonel who captured him, and the clumsy attempt of the rebel officer to establish the contrary, effectually prove it. On the 4th October, 1864, Mr. Davis, speaking of "the Yankees," declared that "the only way to make spaniels civil is to whip them." A few months only had elapsed, and this man who spoke of Northerners as of dogs, was caught by them running away as an old woman with a tin pail. This was the end of the Great Rebellion.

Mr. Raymond declares that "the people had been borne on the top of a lofty wave of joy ever since Sheridan's victory; and the news of Lee's surrender, with Lincoln's return to Washington, intensified the universal exultation." On the 10th April, 1865, an immense crowd assembled at the White House, which was illuminated, as "the whole city also was a-blaze

---

[1] *Vide* Frank Moore's "Rebellion Record," 1864-5—Rumours and Incidents, p. 9.

with bonfires and waving with flags." And on this occasion, so inspired with joy soon to be turned to the deepest grief which ever fell on the nation, Lincoln delivered his last address. Hitherto he had always spoken with hope, but never without pain; after he had for once lifted his voice in joy he never spoke again. In this address he did not exult over the fallen, but discussed the best method of reconstruction, or how to bring the revolted states again into the Union as speedily and as kindly as possible.

No time was lost in relieving the nation from the annoyances attendant on war. Between the 11th April, 1865, and the 15th, proclamations were issued, declaring all drafting and recruiting to be stopped, with all purchases of arms and supplies, removing all military restrictions upon trade and commerce, and opening the blockaded ports. The promptness with which the army returned to peaceful pursuits was, considering its magnitude, unprecedented in history. The grand army mustered over 1,200,000 men. The population of the twenty-three loyal states, including Missouri, Kentucky, and Maryland—which latter state furnished soldiers for both sides, from a population of 3,025,745—was 22,046,472, and this supplied the aggregate, reduced to a three years' standard, of 2,129,041 men, or fourteen and a-half per cent. of the whole population. Ninety-six thousand and eighty-nine died from wounds, 184,331 from disease—total, 280,420—the actual number being more. The cost of the war to the United States was 3,098,233,078 dollars, while the States expended in bounties, or premiums to recruits, 500,000,000 dollars. The blacks furnished their fair proportion of soldiers, and, if suffering and death be a test of courage, a much greater proportion of bravery than the whites, as of 178,975 black troops, 68,178 perished.

Mr. Lincoln's last speech was entirely devoted to a kind consideration of the means by which he might restore their privileges to the rebels; and his last story was a kindly excuse for letting one escape. It was known that Jacob Thompson, a notorious Confederate, meant to escape in disguise. The President, as usual, was disposed to be merciful, and to permit the arch-rebel to pass unmolested, but his Secretary urged that he should be arrested as a traitor. "By permitting him to escape the penalties of treason," remarked the Secretary, "you sanction it." "Well," replied Mr. Lincoln, "that puts me in mind of a little story. There was an Irish soldier last summer who stopped at a chemist's, where he saw a soda-fountain. 'Misther Doctor,' he said, 'give me, plase, a glass ov soda-wather—and if ye can put in a few drops of whiskey unbeknown to anyone, I'll be obleeged till yees.' Now," continued Mr. Lincoln, "if Jake Thompson is permitted to go away unknown to anyone, where's the harm? *Don't* have him arrested."

And now the end was drawing near. As the taper which has burned almost away flashes upwards, as if it would cast its fire-life to heaven, so Abraham Lincoln, when his heart was for once, and once only, glad and light, perished suddenly. During the whole war he had been hearing from many sources that his life was threatened. There were always forming, in the South, Devoted Bands and Brotherhoods of Death, sanctioned by the Confederate Congress, whose object was simply arson, robbery, and murder in the North. Many have forgotten, but I have not, what appeared in the rebel newspapers of those days, or with what the detective police of the North were continually busy. The deeds of Beal and Kennedy,[1] men holding commissions from the authorities of Richmond for the purpose, showed that a government could stoop to attempt to burn hundreds of women and children alive, and throw railway trains full of peaceable citizens off the track. It is to the credit of the North that, in their desire for reconciliation, the question as to who were the instigators and authorisers of Lincoln's death was never pushed very far. The world was satisfied with being told that the murderer was a crazy actor, and the rebels eagerly caught at the idea. But years have now passed, and it is time that the truth should be known. As Dr. Brockett

---

[1] See "Trial and Sentence of Beal and Kennedy," M'Pherson's "Political History," pp. 552, 553.

declares, a plot, the extent and ramifications of which have never yet been fully made known, had long been formed to assassinate the President and the prominent members of the Cabinet. "Originating in the Confederate Government, this act, with others, such as the attempt to fire New York, . . . was confided to an association of army officers, who, when sent on these errands, were said to be on 'detached service.'" There is *direct proof* of Booth's actual consultation with officers known to belong to this organisation, during Lee's retreat from Gettysburg. The assassination of the President was a thing so commonly talked of in the South as to excite no surprise. A reward was actually offered in one of the Southern papers for "the murder of the President, Vice-President, and Secretary Seward." Now when such an offer is followed by such an attempt, few persons would deny the connection. It is true that there were, even among the most zealous Union-men at this time, some whose desire to acquire political influence in the South, and be regarded as conciliators, was so great, that they hastened to protest, as zealously as any rebels, that the Confederate Government had no knowledge of the plot. Perhaps from the depths of Mr. Jefferson Davis's inner conscience there may yet come forth some tardy avowal of the truth. When that gentleman was arrested, he protested that he had done nothing for which he could be punished; but when he heard, in answer, that he might be held accountable for complicity in the murder of President Lincoln, he was silent and seemed alarmed. But the almost conclusive proof that the murder was carried out under the sanction and influence of high authorities, may be found in the great number of people who were engaged in it, and the utter absence among them of those guiding minds which invariably direct conspiracies. When on one night a great number of hotels were fired in New York, the Copperhead press declared that it was done by thieves. But the Fire Marshal of Philadelphia, who was an old detective, said that common incendiaries like burglars never worked in large parties. It was directed by higher authority. Everything in the murder of President Lincoln indicated that the assassin and his accomplices were tools in stronger hands. The rebellion had failed, but the last blow of revenge was struck with unerring Southern vindictiveness. After all, as a question of mere morality, the exploits of Beal and Kennedy show that the Confederate Government had authorised deeds a hundred times more detestable than the simple murder of President Lincoln. Political enthusiasm might have induced thousands to regard Lincoln as a tyrant and Booth as a Brutus; but the most fervent madness of faction can never apologise for burning women and children alive, or killing them on railways.

It was on Good Friday, the 14th of April, the anniversary of Major Anderson's evacuation of Fort Sumter, "the opening scene of the terrible four years' civil war," that President Lincoln was murdered while sitting in a box at a theatre in Washington. The assassin, John Wilkes Booth, was the son of the celebrated actor. He was twenty-seven years of age, and utterly dissipated and eccentric. He was a thorough rebel, and had often exhibited a nickel bullet with which he declared he meant to shoot Lincoln, but his wild and unsteady character had prevented those who heard the threats from attaching importance to them. It had been advertised that President Lincoln and many prominent men would be present at a performance. General Grant, who was to have been of their number, had left that afternoon for Philadelphia. During the day, the assassin and his accomplices, who were all perfectly familiar with the theatre, had carefully made every preparation for the murder. The entrance to the President's box was commanded by a door, and in order to close this, a piece of wood was provided, which would brace against it so firmly that no one could enter. In order to obtain admission, the spring-locks of the doors were weakened by partially withdrawing the screws; so that, even if locked, they could present no resistance. Many other details were most carefully arranged, including those for Booth's escape. He had hired a fine horse, and employed one Spangler, the stage carpenter, to watch it. This man had also prepared the scenes so that he could readily reach the door. In the afternoon he called on Vice-President Johnson, sending up his card, but was denied admission, as that gentleman was busy. It is supposed to have been an act intended to cast suspicion upon Mr. Johnson, who would be Lincoln's successor. At seven o'clock, Booth, with five of his accomplices, entered a saloon, where they drank together in such a manner as to attract attention. All was ready.

President Lincoln had, during the day, held interviews with many distinguished men, and discussed great measures. He had consulted with Colfax, the Speaker of the House, as to his future policy towards the South, and had seen the Minister to Spain, with several senators. At eleven o'clock he had met the Cabinet and General Grant, and held a most important conference. "When it adjourned, Secretary Stanton said he felt that the Government was stronger than it had ever been;" and after this meeting he again conversed with Mr. Colfax and several leading citizens of his own state. His last remarks in reference to public affairs expressed an interest in the development of California, and he promised to send a telegram in reference to it to Mr. Colfax when he should be in San Francisco. As I have, however, stated with reference to Jacob Thompson, his own last act was to save the life, as he supposed, of a rebel, while the last act of the rebellion was to take his own.

At nine o'clock, Lincoln and his wife reached the crowded theatre, and were received with great applause. Then the murderer went to his work. Through the crowd in the rear of the dress circle, patiently and softly, he made his way to the door opening into the dark narrow passage leading to the President's box. Here he showed a card to the servant in attendance, saying that Mr. Lincoln had sent for him, and the man, nothing doubting, admitted him. He entered the vestibule, and secured the door behind him by bracing against it the piece of board already mentioned. He then drew a small silver-mounted Derringer pistol, which he held in his right hand, having a long double-edged dagger in his left. All in the box were absorbed in watching the actors on the stage, except President Lincoln, who was leaning forward, holding aside the flag-curtain of the box with his left hand, with his head slightly turned towards the audience. At this instant Booth passed by the inner door into the box, and stepping softly behind the President, holding the pistol over the chair, shot him through the back of the head. The ball entered on the left side behind the ear, through the brain, and lodged just behind the right eye. President Lincoln made no great movement—his head fell slightly forward, and his eyes closed. He seemed stunned.

As the report of the pistol rang through the house, many of the audience supposed it was part of some new incident introduced into the play. Major Rathbone, who was in the box, saw at once what had occurred, and threw himself on Booth, who dropped the pistol, and freed himself by stabbing his assailant in the arm, near the shoulder. The murderer then rushed to the front of the box, and, in a sharp loud voice, exclaiming, *Sic semper tyrannis*—the motto of Virginia—leaped on the stage below. As he went over, his spur caught in the American flag which Mr. Lincoln had grasped, and he fell, breaking his leg; but, recovering himself, he rose, brandishing the dagger theatrically, and, facing the audience, cried in stage-style, "The South is avenged," and rushed from the theatre. He pushed Miss Laura Keene, the actress, out of his way, ran down a dark passage, pursued by Mr. Stewart, sprung to his saddle, and escaped. Mrs. Lincoln had fainted, the excited audience behaved like lunatics, some attempting to climb up the pillars into the box. Through Miss Keene's presence of mind, the gas was turned down, and the crowd was turned out. And in a minute after, the telegraph had shot all over the United States the news of the murder.

The President never spoke again. He was taken

to his home, and died at twenty minutes after seven the next morning. He was unconscious from the moment he was shot.

As the vast crowd, mad with grief, poured forth, weeping and lamenting, they met with another multitude bringing the news that Secretary Seward, lying on his sick-bed, had been nearly murdered. A few days before, he had fractured his arm and jaw by falling from a carriage. While in this condition, an accomplice of Booth's, named John Payne Powell, tried to enter the room, but was repulsed by Mr. Seward's son, who was at once knocked down with the butt of a pistol. Rushing into the room, Payne Powell stabbed Mr. Seward three times, and escaped, but not before he had wounded, while fighting desperately, five people in all.

During the night, there was fearful excitement in Washington. Rumours were abroad that the President was murdered—that all the members of the Cabinet had perished, or were wounded—that General Grant had barely escaped with his life—that the rebels had risen, and were seizing on Washington—and that all was confusion. The reality was enough to warrant any degree of doubt and terror. There had been, indeed, a conspiracy to murder all the leading members of Government. General Grant had escaped by going to Philadelphia. It is said that this most immovable of men, when he heard that President Lincoln was dead, gravely took the cigar from his mouth and quietly said, "Then I must go at once to Washington. I shall yet have time to take my family to Bordertown, and catch the eleven o'clock train."

Efforts have been made by both parties to confine all the guilt of this murder to Booth alone, and to speak of him as a half-crazed lunatic actor. As the facts stand, the murder had long been threatened by the Southern press, and was apprehended by many people. Booth had so many accomplices, that they expected between them to kill the President, Vice-President, and all the Cabinet. And yet, with every evidence of a widespread conspiracy which had numbers of ready and shrewd agents in the theatre, on the road, and far and wide, even the most zealous Union writers have declared that all this plot had its beginning and end in the brain of a lunatic! It so happened that, just at this time, the North, weary of war and willing to pardon every enemy, had no desire to be vindictive. When Jefferson Davis was tried, Mr. Greeley eagerly stepped forward to be his bail, and there were many more looking to reconstruction and reconciliation—or to office—and averse to drive the foe to extremes. Perhaps they were right; for in great emergencies minor interests must be forgotten. It was the Union-men and the victors who were now nobly calling for peace at any price and forgiveness.

But one thing is at least certain. From a letter found April 15th, 1865, in Booth's trunk, it was shown that the murder was planned before the 4th of March, but fell through then because the accomplices refused to go further *until Richmond could be heard from*. So it appears that, though Booth was regarded as the beginning and end of the plot, and solely accountable, yet his tools actually refused to obey him until they had heard from Richmond, the seat of the Rebel Government. This was written by Secretary Stanton to General Dix on April 15th, in the interval between the attack on Lincoln and his death. The entire execution of the plot evidently depended upon *news from Richmond*, and not upon Booth's orders.

Booth himself, escaping across the Potomac, "found, for some days, shelter and aid among the rebel sympathisers of Lower Maryland." He was, of course, pursued, and, having taken refuge in a barn, was summoned to surrender. This he refused to do, and was then shot dead by a soldier named Boston Corbett, whom I have heard described as a fanatic of the old Puritan stamp. In the words of Arnold, Booth did not live to betray the men who set him on. And I can testify that there was nowhere much desire to push the inquiry *too* far. Booth had been shot, the leading Union politicians were busy at reconstruction, and the war was at an end. But, as Arnold declares, tools of the real conspirators, and it remains uncertain whether the conspirators themselves will ever in this world be dragged to light.

The next day, April 15th, 1865, the whole nation knew the dreadful news, and there was such universal sadness as had never been known within the memory of man. All was gloom and mourning; men walked in the public places, and wept aloud as if they had been alone; women sat with children on the steps of houses, wailing and sobbing. Strangers stopped to converse and cry. I saw in that day more of the human heart than in all the rest of my life. I saw in Philadelphia a great mob surging idly here and there between madness and grief, not knowing what to do. Somebody suggested that the Copperheads were rejoicing over the murder—as they indeed were—and so the mob attacked their houses, but soon gave it over, out of very despondency. By common sympathy, every family began to dress their houses in mourning, and to hang black stuff in all the public places; "before night, the whole nation was shrouded in black." That day I went from Philadelphia to Pittsburg. This latter town, owing to its factories and immense consumption of bituminous coal, seems at any time as if in mourning; but on that Sunday afternoon, completely swathed and hung in black, with all the world weeping in a drizzling rain, its dolefulness grief was very great; but with the poor negroes, it was absolute—I may say that to them the murder was in reality a second crucifixion, since, in their religious enthusiasm, they literally believed the President to be a Saviour appointed by God to lead them forth to freedom. To this day there are negro huts, especially in Cuba, where Lincoln's portrait is preserved as a hidden fetish, and as the picture of the Great Prophet who was not killed, but only taken away, and who will come again, like King Arthur, to lead his people to liberty. At Lincoln's funeral, the weeping of the coloured folk was very touching.

It was proposed that President Lincoln should be buried in the vault originally constructed for Washington in the Capitol. This would have been most appropriate; but the representatives from Illinois were very urgent that his remains should be taken to his native state, and this was finally done. So, after funeral services in Washington, the body was borne with sad processions from city to city, through Maryland, Pennsylvania, New Jersey, New York, Ohio, Indiana, and Illinois. At Philadelphia it lay in state in the hall where the declaration of Independence had been signed. "A half-million of people were in the streets to do honour to all that was left of him who, in that same hall, had declared, four years before, that he would sooner be assassinated than give up the principles of the Declaration of Independence. He *had* been assassinated because he would not give them up."

This death-journey, with its incidents, was very touching. It showed beyond all question that, during his Presidency, the Illinois backwoodsman had found his way to the hearts of the people as no man had ever done. He had been with them in their sorrows and their joys. Those who had wept in the family circle for a son or father lost in the war, now wept again the more because the great chief had also perished. The last victim of the war was its leader.

The final interment of the body of President Lincoln took place at Oak Ridge Cemetery, in Springfield, Illinois. Four years previously, Abraham Lincoln had left a little humble home in that place, and gone to be tried by the people in such a great national crisis as seldom falls to any man to meet. He had indeed "crossed Fox River" in such a turmoil of roaring waters as had never been dreamed of. And, having done all things wisely and well, he passed away with the war, dying with its last murmurs.

CHAPTER XIII.

President Lincoln's Characteristics—His Love of Humour—His Stories—Pithy Sayings—Repartees—His Dignity.

WHATEVER the defects of Lincoln's character were, it may be doubted whether there was ever so great a man who was, on the whole, so good, Compared to his better qualities, these faults were as nothing; yet they came forth so boldly, owing to the natural candour and manliness on which they grew, that, to petty minds, they obscured what was grand and beautiful. It has been very truly said, that he was the most remarkable product of the remarkable possibilities of American life. Born to extreme poverty, and with fewer opportunities for culture than are open to any British peasant, he succeeded, by sheer perseverance and determination, in making himself a land-surveyor, a lawyer, a politician, and a President. And it is not less evident that even his honesty was the result of *will*, though his kind-heartedness came by nature. What was most remarkable in him was his thorough Republicanism. He was so completely inspired with a sense that the opinions and interests common to the community are right, that to his mind common sense assumed its deepest meaning as a rule of the highest justice. When the whole land was a storm of warring elements, and in the strife between States' Rights and National Supremacy all precedents were forgotten and every man made his own law, then Abraham Lincoln, watching events, and guided by what he felt was really the sense of the people, sometimes leading, but always following when he could, achieved Emancipation, and brought a tremendous civil war to a quiet end.

Abraham Lincoln was remarkably free from jealousy or personal hatred. His honesty in all things, great or small, was most exemplary. In appointing men, he was more guided by the interests of the country or their fitness than by any other consideration, and avoided favouritism to such an extent that it was once said, in reference to him, that honesty was undoubtedly good policy, but it was hard that an American citizen should be excluded from office because he had, unfortunately, at some time been a friend of the President. Owing to this principle, he was often accused of ingratitude, heartlessness, or indifference. Mr. Lincoln had a quick perception of character, and liked to give men credit for what they understood. Once, when his opinion was asked as to politics, he said, "You must ask Raymond about that; in politics, he is my lieutenant-general."[1] The manner in which Lincoln became gradually appreciated was well expressed in the London "Saturday Review," after his death, when it said that, "during the arduous experience of four years, Mr. Lincoln constantly rose in general estimation by calmness of temper, by an intuitively logical appreciation of the character of the conflict, and by undisputed sincerity."

Mr. Lincoln was habitually very melancholy, and, as is often the case, sought for a proper balance of mind in the humour of which he had such a rare appreciation. When he had a great duty on hand, he would prepare his mind for it by reading "something funny." As I write this, I am kindly supplied with an admirable illustration by Mr. Bret Harte. One evening the President, who had summoned his Cabinet at a most critical juncture, instead of proceeding to any business, passed half-an-hour in reading to them the comic papers of Orpheus C. Kerr (office-seeker), which had just appeared. But at last, when more than one gentleman was little less than offended at such levity, Mr. Lincoln rose, laid aside the book, and, with a most serious air, as of one who has brought his mind to a great point, produced and read the slips containing the Proclamation of Emancipation, and this he did with an earnestness and feeling which were

---

[1] The late Henry J. Raymond, then editor of the New York "Times."

electric, moving his auditors as they had seldom been moved. By far the best work of humour produced during the war, if it be not indeed the best work of purely American humour ever written, was the Petroleum V. Nasby papers. F. B. Carpenter relates that, on the Saturday before the President left Washington to go to Richmond, he had a most wearisome day, followed by an interview with several callers on business of great importance. Pushing everything aside, he said—"Have you seen the 'Nasby Papers'?" "No, I have not," was the answer; "what are they?" "There is a chap out in Ohio," returned the President, "who has been writing a series of letters in the newspapers over the signature of Petroleum V. Nasby. Some one sent me a collection of them the other day. I am going to write to Petroleum to come down here, and I intend to tell him, if he will communicate his talent to me, I will swap places with him." Thereupon he arose, went to a drawer in his desk, and taking out the letters, he sat down and read one to the company, finding in their enjoyment of it the temporary excitement and relief which another man would have found in a glass of wine. The moment he ceased, the book was thrown aside, his countenance relapsed into its habitual serious expression, and business was entered upon with the utmost earnestness. The author of these "Nasby Papers" was David R. Locke. After Mr. Lincoln's death, two comic works, both well thumbed, indicating that they had been much read, were found in his desk. One was the "Nasby Letters," and the other "The Book of Copperheads," written and illustrated by myself and my brother, the late Henry P. Leland. This was kindly lent to me by Mr. M'Pherson, Clerk of the House of Representatives, that I might see how thoroughly Mr. Lincoln had read it. Both of these works were satires on that party in the North which sympathised with the South.

Men of much reading, and with a varied knowledge of life, especially if their minds have somewhat of critical culture, draw their materials for illustration in conversation from many sources. Abraham Lincoln's education and reading were not such as to supply him with much unworn or refined literary illustration, so he used such material as he had—incidents and stories from the homely life of the West. I have observed that, in Europe, Scotchmen approach most nearly to Americans in this practical application of events and anecdotes. Lincoln excelled in the art of putting things aptly and concisely, and, like many old Romans, would place his whole argument in a brief droll narrative, the point of which would render his whole meaning clear to the dullest intellect. In their way, these were like the illustrated proverbs known as fables. Menenius Agrippa and Lincoln would have been congenial spirits. However coarse or humble the illustration might be, Mr. Lincoln never failed to convince even the most practised diplomatists or lawyers that he had a marvellous gift for grasping rapidly all the details of a difficulty, and for reducing this knowledge to a practical deduction, and, finally, for presenting the result in a concisely humorous illustration which impressed it on the memory.

Mr. Lincoln was in a peculiar way an original thinker, without being entirely an originator, as a creative genius is. His stories were seldom or never his own inventions; hundreds of them were well known, but, in the words of Dr. Thompson. "however common his ideas were to other minds, however simple when stated, they bore the stamp of individuality, and became in some way his own." During his life, and within a few months after his death, I made a large MS. collection of Lincolniana. Few of the stories were altogether new, but most were original in application. It is said that, being asked if a very stingy neighbour of his was a man of *means*, Mr. Lincoln replied that he ought to be, for he was about the *meanest* man round there. This may or may not be authentic, but it is eminently Lincolnian. So with the jests of Tyll Eulenspiegel, or of any other great droll; he invariably becomes the nucleus of a certain kind of humour.

Unconsciously, Abraham Lincoln became a great proverbialist. Scores of his pithy sayings are current among the people. "In giving freedom to the slave, we assure freedom to the free," is the sum-total of all the policy which urged Emancipation for the sake of the white man. "This struggle of to-day is for a vast future also," expressed a great popular opinion. "We are making history rapidly," was very flattering to all who shared in the war. "If slavery is not wrong, *nothing* is wrong," spoke the very extreme of conviction. The whole people took his witty caution "not to swap horses in the middle of a stream." When it was always urged by the Democrats that emancipation implied amalgamation, he answered—"I do not understand that because I do not want a negro woman for a slave, I must necessarily want her for a wife." This popular Democratic shibboleth, "How would you like your daughter to marry a negro?" was keenly satirised by Nasby. I have myself known a Democratic procession in Philadelphia to contain a car with a parcel of girls dressed in white, and the motto, "Fathers, protect us from Black Husbands." To which the Republican banner simply replied, "*Our* Daughters do not want to marry Black Husbands."

Abraham Lincoln was always moderate in argument. Once, when Judge Douglas attempted to parry an argument by impeaching the veracity of a senator whom Mr. Lincoln had quoted, he answered that the question was not one of veracity, but simply one of argument. He said—"Euclid, by a course of reasoning, proves that all the angles in a triangle are equal to two right angles ; now, would you undertake to disprove that assertion by calling Euclid a liar?"

"I never did invent anything original—I am only a *retail dealer*," is very characteristic of Mr. Lincoln. He was speaking of the stories credited to him, and yet the modesty of the remark, coupled with the droll distinction between original wholesale manufacturers and retail dealers, is both original and quaint.

Mr. Lincoln was very ingenious in finding reasons for being merciful. On one occasion, a young soldier who had shown himself very brave in war, and had been severely wounded, after a time deserted. Being re-captured, he was under sentence of death, and President Lincoln was of course petitioned for his pardon. It was a difficult case ; the young man deserved to die, and desertion was sadly injuring the army. The President mused solemnly, until a happy thought struck him. "Did you say he was once badly wounded?" he asked of the applicant for a pardon. "He was." "Then, as the Scripture says that in the shedding of blood is the remission of sins, I guess we'll have to let him off this time."

When Mr. Lincoln was grossly and foolishly flattered, as happened once in the case of a gushing "interviewer," who naïvely put his own punishment into print, he could quiz the flatterer with great ingenuity by apparently falling into the victim's humour. When only moderately praised, he retorted gently. Once, when a gentleman complimented him on having no vices, such as drinking or smoking, "That is a doubtful compliment," answered Mr. Lincoln. "I recollect once being outside a stage-coach in Illinois, when a man offered me a cigar. I told him I had no vices. He said nothing, but smoked for some time, and then growled out, 'It's my opinion that people who have no vices have plaguy few virtues."

President Lincoln was not merely obliging or condescending in allowing every one to see him; in his simple Republicanism, he believed that the people who had made him President had a right to talk to him. One day a friend found him half-amused, half-irritated. "You met an old lady as you entered," he said. "Well, she wanted me to give her an order for stopping the pay of a Treasury clerk who owes her a board-bill of seventy dollars." His visitor expressed surprise that he did not adopt the usual military plan, under which every application to see the general commanding had to be filtered through a sieve of officers, who allowed no one to take up the chief's time except those who had business of sufficient importance. "Ah yes," the President replied, "such things may do very well for you military people, with your arbitrary rule. But the office of a President is a very different one, and the affair is very different. For myself, I feel, though the tax on my time is heavy, that no hours of my day are better employed than those which thus bring me again into direct contact with the people. All serves to renew in me a clearer and more vivid image of that great popular assemblage out of which I sprung, and to which, at the end of two years, I must return." To such an extreme did he carry this, and such weariness did it cause him, that, at the end of four years, he who had been one of the strongest men living, was no longer strong or vigorous. But he always had a good-natured story, even for his tormentors. Once, when a Kentucky farmer wanted him at a critical period of the Emancipation question to exert himself and turn the whole machinery of government to aid him in recovering two slaves, President Lincoln said this reminded him of Jack Chase, the captain of a western steamboat. It is a terrible thing to steer a boat down the roaring rapids, where the mistake of an inch may cause wreck, and it requires the extreme attention of the pilot. One day, when the boat was plunging and wallowing along the boiling current, and Jack at the wheel was using all care to keep in the perilous channel, a boy pulled his coat-tail and cried, "Say, Mister Captain! I wish you'd stop your boat a minute. *I've lost my apple overboard.*"

In self-conscious "dėportment," Mr. Lincoln was utterly deficient; in true unconscious *dignity*, he was unsurpassed. He would sit down on the stone-coping outside the White House to write on his card the directions by which a poor man might be relieved from his sorrow, looking as he did so as if he were sitting on the pavement; or he would actually lie down on the grass beside a common soldier, and go over his papers with him, while his carriage waited, and great men gathered around; but no man ever dared to be impertinent, or unduly familiar with him. Once an insolent officer accused him to his face of injustice, and he arose, lifted the man by the collar, and carried him out, kicking. But this is, I believe, the only story extant of any one having treated him with insolence.

Hunting popularity by means of petty benevolence is so usual with professional politicians, that many may suspect that Lincoln was not unselfish in his acts of kindness. But I myself know of one instance of charity exercised by him, which was certainly most disinterested. One night, a poor old man, whose little farm had been laid waste during the war, and who had come to Washington, hoping that Government would repay his loss, found himself penniless in the streets of the capital. A person whom I know very well saw him accost the President, who listened to his story, and then, writing something on a piece of paper, gave it to him, and with it a ten-dollar note. The President went his way, and my acquaintance going up to the old man, who was deeply moved, asked him what was the matter. "I thank God," said the old man, using a quaint American phrase, "that there are some *white* people [1] in this town. I've been tryin' to get somebody to listen to me, and nobody would, because I'm a poor foolish old body. But just now a stranger listened to all my story, and give me this here." He said this, showing the money and the paper, which contained a request to Secretary Stanton to have the old man's claim investigated at once, and, if just, promptly satisfied. When it is remembered that Lincoln went into office and out of it a poor man, or at least a very poor man for one in his position, his frequent acts of charity appear doubly creditable.

Whatever may be said of Lincoln, he was always simply and truly *a good man.* He was a good father to his children, and a good President to the people, whom he loved as if they had been his children. America and the rest of the world have had many great rulers, but never one who, like Lincoln, was so much one of the people, or who was so sympathetic in their sorrows and trials.

---

[1] "White people"—civilised, decent, kind-hearted people.

APPENDIX.

[FROM THE NEW YORK EVENING POST, AUGUST 16, 1867.]

HIS LECTURE AT THE COOPER INSTITUTE IN 1860.

To the Editor of The Evening Post:

IN October, 1859, Messrs. Joseph H. Richards, J. M. Pettingill, and S. W. Tubbs called on me at the office of the Ohio Trade Agency, 25 William Street, and requested me to write to the Hon. Thomas Corwin of Ohio, and the Hon. Abraham Lincoln of Illinois, and invite them to lecture in a course of lectures these young gentlemen proposed for the winter in Plymouth Church, Brooklyn.

I wrote the letters as requested, and offered as compensation for each lecture, as I was authorized, the sum of $200. The proposition to lecture was accepted by Messrs. Corwin and Lincoln. Mr. Corwin delivered his lecture in Plymouth Church, as he was on his way to Washington to attend Congress; Mr. Lincoln could not lecture until late in the season, and the proposition was agreed to by the gentlemen named, and accepted by Mr. Lincoln, as the following letter will show:

"DANVILLE, ILLINOIS, *November* 13, 1859.
"JAMES A. BRIGGS, ESQ.

"DEAR SIR: Yours of the 1st inst., closing with my proposition for compromise, was duly received. I will be on hand, and in due time will notify you of the exact day. I believe, after all, I shall make a political speech of it. You have no objection?

"I would like to know in advance, whether I am also to speak in New York.

"Very, very glad your election went right.

"Yours truly,

"A. LINCOLN.

"P.S.—I am here at court, but my address is still at Springfield, Ill."

In due time Mr. Lincoln wrote me that he would deliver the lecture, a political one, on the evening of the 27th of February, 1860. This was rather late in the season for a lecture, and the young gentlemen who were responsible were doubtful about its success, as the expenses were large. It was stipulated that the lecture was to be in Plymouth Church, Brooklyn; I requested and urged that the lecture should be delivered at the Cooper Institute. They were fearful it would not pay expenses—$350. I thought it would.

In order to relieve Messrs. Richards, Pettingill, and Tubbs of all responsibility, I called upon some of the officers of "The Young Men's Republican Union," and proposed that they should take Mr. Lincoln, and that the lecture should be delivered under their auspices. They respectfully declined.

I next called upon Mr. Simeon Draper, then president of "The Draper Republican Union Club of New York," and proposed to him that his "Union" take Mr. Lincoln and the lecture, and assume the responsibility of the expenses. Mr. Draper and his friends declined, and Mr. Lincoln was left on the hands of "the original Jacobs."

After considerable discussion, it was agreed on the part of the young gentlemen that the lecture should be delivered in the Cooper Institute, if I would agree to share one-fourth of the expenses, if the sale of the tickets (25 cents) for the lecture did not meet the outlay. To this I assented, and the lecture was advertised to be delivered in the Cooper Institute, on the evening of the 27th of February.

Mr. Lincoln read the notice of the lecture in the papers, and, without any knowledge of the arrangement, was somewhat surprised to learn that he was first to make his appearance before a New York audience, instead of a Plymouth Church audience. A notice of the proposed lecture appeared in the New York papers, and the *Times* spoke of him "as a lawyer who had some local reputation in Illinois."

At my personal solicitation MR. WILLIAM CULLEN BRYANT presided as chairman of the meeting, and introduced Mr. Lincoln for the first time to a New York audience.

The lecture was a wonderful success; it has become a part of the history of the country. Its remarkable ability was everywhere acknowledged, and after the 27th of February the name of Mr. Lincoln was a familiar one to all the people of the East. After Mr. Lincoln closed his lecture, Mr. David Dudley Field, Mr. James W. Nye, Mr. Horace Greeley, and myself were called out by the audience and made short speeches. I remember of saying then, "One of three gentlemen will be our standard-bearer in the presidential contest of this year: the distinguished Senator of New York, Mr. Seward; the late able and accomplished Governor of Ohio, Mr. Chase; or the 'Unknown Knight' who entered the political lists against the Bois Guilbert of Democracy on the prairies of Illinois in 1858, and unhorsed him—Abraham Lincoln." Some friends joked me after the meeting as not being a "good prophet." The lecture was over—all the expenses were paid, and I was handed by the gentlemen interested the sum of $4.25 as my share of the profits, as they would have called on me if there had been a deficiency in the receipts to meet the expenses.

Immediately after the lecture, Mr. Lincoln went to Exeter, N. H., to visit his son Robert, then at school there, and I sent him a check for $200. Mr. Tubbs informed me a few weeks ago that after the check was paid at the Park Bank he tore it up; but that he would give $200 for the check if it could be restored with the endorsement of "A. Lincoln," as it was made payable to the order of Mr. Lincoln.

After the return of Mr. Lincoln to New York from the East, where he had made several speeches, he said to me, "I have seen what all the New York papers said about that thing of mine in the Cooper Institute, with the exception of the New York *Evening Post*, and I would like to know what Mr. Bryant thought of it;" and he then added, "It is worth a visit from Springfield, Illinois, to New York to make the acquaintance of such a man as WILLIAM CULLEN

BRYANT." At Mr. Lincoln's request, I sent him a copy of the *Evening Post* with a notice of his lecture.

On returning from Mr. Beecher's Church, on Sunday, in company with Mr. Lincoln, as we were passing the post-office, I remarked to him, "Mr. Lincoln, I wish you would take particular notice of what a dark and dismal place we have here for a post-office, and I do it for this reason: I think your chance for being the next President is equal to that of any man in the country. When you are President will you recommend an appropriation of a million of dollars for a suitable location for a post-office in this city?" With a significant gesture Mr. Lincoln remarked, "I will make a note of that."

On going up Broadway with Mr. Lincoln in the evening, from the Astor House, to hear the Rev. Dr. E. H. Chapin, he said to me, "When I was East several gentlemen made about the same remarks to me that you did to-day about the Presidency; they thought my chances were about equal to the best."

JAMES A. BRIGGS.

N.B.—The writers of Mr. Lincoln's Biography have things considerably mixed about Mr. Lincoln going to the Five Points Mission School, at the Five Points, in New York, that he found his way there alone, etc., etc. Mr. Lincoln went there in the afternoon with his old friend Hiram Burney, Esq., and after Mr. B. had informed Mr. Barlow, the Superintendent, who the stranger with him was, Mr. Barlow requested Mr. Lincoln to speak to the children, which he did. I met Mr. Lincoln at Mr. Burney's at tea, just after this pleasant, and to him strange, visit at the Five Points Mission School.

J. A. B.

INDEX.

ABOLITIONISM, 49, 66, 122, 126, 168.
Alabama, 145, 196.
Anti-slavery protest, 48, 50, 51; resolutions, 59.

BALDWIN, JOHN, the smith, 27.
Barbarities, 186.
Black regiment, charge of the, 161.
Black's (Judge) decision, 93.
Blockade declared, 108.
Booth, his plans, 221; antecedents, 223; death, 229.
Border ruffians and outrages, 68, 69, 71.
Buchanan, President, 92.
Bull Run, 113, 114.
Burnside, General, 142.

CABINET, treason in the, 92.
Chancellorsville, battle of, 148.
Chattanooga, battle of, 164.
Clay, Henry, 57.
Compromises of 1826 and 1850, 65.
Confederate organisation in Europe, 117; agents in Canada, 197; proposals, 205.
Conspiracies, suspected, 88.
Copperheads, 96, 179; book of, 237.
Colonisation of slaves proposed, 123.
Cost of the war, 219.

DAVIS, JEFFERSON, President of Confederacy, 94, 109; escape of, 217.
"Dred Scott" decision, 73.
Douglas, Stephen, 47, 67, 69, 70, 74, 77, 84, 110.

ELLSWORTH and Winthrop, death of, 112.

Enlistment of coloured troops, 133.
Exhaustive effects of Northern incursions, 185.

FARRAGUT, Admiral, 194.
Fox River anecdote, 95.
Fremont, 73, 169.

GETTYSBURG, battle of, 150.
Gloom of 1863, 179.
Grant, "Unconditional Surrender," 137; daring march, 157; succession of victories, 158; last battle, 212; chase of Lee, 215.
Greeley, Horace, 79.

HANKS, NANCY, 9, 12, 15.
Hood, General, 188.
Hooker, General, 187.
Hicks, Governor, and Maryland, 107, 108.

JACKSON, death of General Stonewall, 149.
Johnston, Mrs., Lincoln's second mother, 18–20.
Jones of Gentryville, 26.

KANSAS-NEBRASKA Bill, 67.
Kidnapping negroes (note), 67.

LECOMPTON Constitution, 74.
Lincoln, Mordecai and Abraham, 10.
Lincoln, Thomas, his character, 12; his marriage, 15.
Lincoln, Abraham, his family, 9, 10; birth and birth-place, 9; grandfather killed by Indians, 11; schools, 15; migrations, 16, 30; hereditary traits, 13; poverty and

privations, 17; education, 20; death of his mother, 18; acts as ferry-man, 25; characteristics and habits in youth, 21, 22, 23, 25; physical strength, 26, 33; early literary efforts, 27; temperance, 26; earns a dollar, 29; personal appearance, 31; first public speech, 31; splitting rails, 31; postmaster, 43; Black Hawk Indian war—a captain—quells a mutiny, 35-38; love affairs, 45, 54; entrance into political life, 41; becomes a merchant, and studies law, 42; surveying studies, 43; legal experiences, 61, 62, 63; personal popularity, 57; elected to legislature, 44, 45, 70; removal to Springfield, and practice of law, 53; generosity, 57; enters Congress—first speech, 58; Presidential candidate, 54; declines nomination to the Senate, 70; "house-divided-against-itself" speech, 75; nomination for Presidency, 79, 80, 81, 82; lectures in New York and England, 79, 80, 81; elected President, 85; address at Springfield, 89; inaugural speech, 97; first Cabinet, 100; wise forbearance, 103; his mercy, 172, 175; second election, 199; assassination, 225; death, 227; funeral procession, 231; lying in state, 231; interment, 232; general summary of character, 233-244; wit and humour, 240, 241, 242.
Long Nine, the, 46, 47.

Mason and Slidell affair, 131.
M'Clellan, General, 115; apathy of, 140.
Merrimac, the, 141.

Mexican war, 59.
Mexico, the French in, 167.

Nasby, Petroleum V., 236.
Negroes, reception of, 204.

Pea Ridge, battle of, 138.
Port Hudson, surrender of, 162.
Privations in the South, 185.
Proclamation of April 15, 1861, 105.
Prosperity of the North, 180.

Quantrill's guerillas, 170.

Rebellion, breaking out of, 91, 94; progress of, 111.
Religion and irreligion, 55, 56.
Republican party, origin of, 72.
Richmond, fall of, 213.
Riot in New York, 165.

Sanitary fairs, 182.
Secession, 86, 87, 93.
Seward, W. A., refuses to meet the Rebel Commissioners, 102.
Sherman's march, 188, 193.
Shiloh, battle of, 138.
Slavery—slave trade, 103; argument against, 71; slave party, 64, 65.
Sumter, fall of Fort, 104.
Surrender of Confederate forces, 216.

Tennessee, the campaign in, 163.
Todd, Mary, 55.

Union troops attacked, 106.

Virginia's secession, 109, 115.

War, organisation of, 113.
Wilderness, battle of the, 192.
Wilmot's proviso, 66.

THE NEW PLUTARCH.

Lives of men and women of action.

12MO. PRICE, $1.00 PER VOLUME

ABRAHAM LINCOLN; THE ABOLITION OF SLAVERY. With a Portrait. By CHARLES G. LELAND.

COLIGNY; THE FAILURE OF THE FRENCH REFORMATION. With a Portrait. By WALTER BESANT, M.A.

JUDAS MACCABÆUS AND THE JEWISH WAR OF INDEPENDENCE. By CLAUDE REIGNIER CONDER, R.E.

VICTOR EMMANUEL; THE ATTAINMENT OF ITALIAN UNITY. By EDWARD DICEY, M.A.

JOAN OF ARC; THE EXPULSION OF THE ENGLISH FROM FRANCE. By JANET TUCKEY.

ALEXANDER THE GREAT AND HIS AGE; By Rev. W. J. BRODRIBB, M.A.

THE CALIPH HAROUN AL RASCHID; SARACEN CIVILIZATION. By Prof. E. H. PALMER. M.A.

RICHELIEU AND HIS COURT; By WALTER HERRIES POLLOCK, M.A.

HANNIBAL AND CARTHAGINIAN CIVILISATION. By SAMUEL LEE, M.A

HAROLD FAIR HAIR AND THE SCANDINAVIANS. By ERIK MAGNÚSSON, M.A.

CHARLEMAGNE AND HIS TIME. By PROF. BEESLEY.

GUSTAVUS ADOLPHUS. By RICHARD GARNETT.

WHITTINGTON, LORD MAYOR OF LONDON. By JAMES RICE.

G. P. PUTNAM'S SONS,
182 FIFTH AVENUE, NEW YORK.

www.ingramcontent.com/pod-product-compliance
Lightning Source LLC
Chambersburg PA
CBHW020759230426
43666CB00007B/771